Chasing Diets

Stop the Endless Search and Discover the Solution

by

Robert Ziltzer, MD
Craig Primack, MD

TELEMACHUS PRESS

Please note: All of the stories you are about to read are accurate and based on real-life stories. In most cases (and with the permission of our patients) we have used their names and stories verbatim. In some cases, we have changed the names or used composites of patients' histories. Most importantly, we have preserved the privacy of our patients while conveying the essential elements for the benefit of our readers.

CHASING DIETS: Stop the Endless Search and Discover the Solution

Copyright © 2019 Robert Ziltzer, MD and Craig Primack, MD All rights reserved, including the right to reproduce this book, or portions thereof, in any form. No part of this text may be reproduced, transmitted, downloaded, decompiled, reverse engineered, or stored in or introduced into any information storage and retrieval system, in any form or by any means, whether electronic or mechanical without the express written permission of the author. The scanning, uploading, and distribution of this book via the Internet or via any other means without the permission of the author and publisher is illegal and punishable by law. Please purchase only authorized electronic editions and do not participate in or encourage electronic piracy of copyrighted materials.

The publisher does not have any control over and does not assume any responsibility for author or third-party websites or their content.

Cover designed by Telemachus Press, LLC

Cover art:
Copyright © iStock/153835746/Jezperklauzen
Copyright © iStock/155600744/Kerrick
Copyright © iStock/170616074/Weekend Images Inc.

Interior illustrations by Jennifer Siegel
Thumbs Up and Down icons Copyright © iStock/622800614/dikobraziy

South Beach Diet is a registered trademark of SBD Enterprises, LLC

Published by Telemachus Press, LLC
7652 Sawmill Road, Suite 304
Dublin, Ohio 43016
http://www.telemachuspress.com

Visit the author website:
http://www.ScottsdaleWeightLoss.com

ISBN: 978-1-948046-33-6 (eBook)
ISBN: 978-1-948046-34-3 (Paperback)
ISBN: 978-1-948046-40-4 (Hard Cover)

Library of Congress Control Number: 2018968539

Health & Fitness / Diet & Nutrition / Weight Loss

Version 2019.01.13

Praise For Chasing Diets

"Obesity is a chronic disease controlled by physiology. Trying to control physiology with behavior is something people can do temporarily, but over the long term, stresses of life get in the way and the weight lost by dieting alone is regained. Long-term control of body weight involves changing physiology in addition to prescribing a diet and changing behavior through increased activity and education. Craig Primack and Robert Ziltzer are diplomates of the American Board of Obesity Medicine. That means that they are physicians with certification in the treatment of obesity as a medical specialty. Thus, they are able to prescribe medications that will change the physiology and enable their patients to have long-term success with diet, education and exercise that would not be possible with diet alone. This makes Chasing Diets not just another diet book, but rather a recipe for success in long-term weight loss that can only be achieved with the help of obesity medicine specialist physicians who have the education and ability to combine all four essential elements needed for long-term weight loss success, medication, education, activity and diet. I recommend this book to those with weight problems looking for a long-term solution"

Frank Greenway, MD
Medical Director and Professor
Pennington Biomedical Research Center
Baton Rouge, Louisiana

"This book by Drs. Ziltzer and Primack illustrates how the complex disease of obesity is effectively treated with coordinated obesity care instead of chasing the latest diet trend. Treating obesity with lifelong sustainable changes, medications, and surgery takes a village. This book is the map to that village. If you are a provider that cares for patients, an employer with employees or a person that has obesity you should read this book."

Angela Fitch, MD
Associate Director,
Massachusetts General Hospital Weight Center
Assistant Professor, Harvard Medical School

"Drs. Ziltzer and Primack have done what most have dared not even attempt...instead of promoting an overly simplified and limited perspective on how obesity should be clinically treated, they have taken on the task of explaining a very challenging and complex issue in an engaging style. One of the reasons we struggle with turning the obesity epidemic around is that we are an immediate gratification society, looking for the latest quick fix. In this book, Rob and

Craig systematically explain why that strategy leaves you feeling unsuccessful and how engaging with a specialist who can individually tailor treatment for you is the way to deal with a complex disease like obesity. This is a clear and honest assessment of what a patient looking for medical weight loss treatment can achieve in partnership with a trained specialist and their team"

Jamy Ard, MD
Professor, Epidemiology and Prevention
Wake Forrest School of Medicine

"Chasing Diets brings a message of hope to those who have tried it all and still find lasting weight loss to be an elusive goal. You are not the problem. Our culture's expectation that weight loss is simply a matter of getting more willpower to eat less and move more is deeply flawed. With deep compassion and scientific rigor, Drs. Ziltzer and Primack offer a compelling argument that perhaps the answer lies in our willingness to view the road to weight loss and well-being as a journey best undertaken with the help of experts who can find solutions that you may not come to on your own. This book's insights and stories will inspire those who are truly ready to get off the diet/weight gain roller coaster for good."

Lisa Galper, PsyD
Clinical Psychologist/Emotional Eating Specialist

"Most doctors do not know how to help you lose weight—because they received no training in weight loss. Drs. Ziltzer and Primack received special training in Obesity Medicine and now that is all they do. I'm confident that the wisdom in these pages, gleaned from years of experience, will help many others!"

Eric C. Westman, MD MHS
Duke University Medical Center
Past President, Obesity Medicine Association
New York Times Bestselling Author of *The New Atkins for a New You*

"There's never enough time to find out what you need and want to know about weight loss, and heaven knows there's an enormous amount of conflicting information and options on the market. This book provides you with the details and the plan from experts you can trust."

Lyn St James
Professional racecar driver
Indianapolis 500 Rookie of the Year, 1992

"As a practicing sleep specialist, *Chasing Diets* is the clear choice for my patients who are serious about making a permanent change in their lives. When it comes to their weight, Drs. Ziltzer and Primack are incredibly knowledgeable, extremely well trained, and include every aspect of your life to ensure success.

So few specialists ever bring all of their thoughts in one place to really give a person value for their time and efforts while trying to accomplish what sometimes seems like an impossible goal. The reason I know so much about this area is not only my expertise in sleep and weight loss (which they expertly address in the book), but I was also a patient. I have maintained my weight loss for the past 8 years, and it has truly changed my life; and the way I think, act, and live."

Michael J. Breus, PhD
aka The Sleep Doctor

Disclaimer

This book is intended to provide readers with information about obesity—symptoms, causes and treatment options. It is not intended to be a prescription for your weight loss program or to be a substitute for professional medical advice or help. Before engaging in any weight loss program, always seek the help of a trained professional who can evaluate your specific situation and design a program around your specific needs and overall health condition. The weight loss examples in this book are real but your results may vary.

Acknowledgments

I want to thank the many people who made this book possible. There are too many to mention them all. Thanks to Jennifer Siegel for her terrific drawings, the staff at Scottsdale Weight Loss Center (SWLC) who make coming to work each day a joy and transformational process for our patients; Lisa Galper, PsyD, for teaching us most of what we know about emotional eating and food addiction; and to my patients who trust in me to lead them along this journey. Ryan and Andie, thank you for bringing me joy and the ability to watch you grow into kind, funny, intelligent and caring adults. Yes, you are now adults. Vivian, I thank you for allowing me to take risks to move to this great career; for your constant support and love. You are my perfect complement.

I want to thank my mom for teaching me the value of education, hard work, and independence.

I so appreciate my dad, who died much too young. Through his quick wit, I learned the value of humor. While in college in the early 1980s, my dad, aged 52, experienced chest pain prompting him to be admitted to the intensive care unit. At that time, medicine did not have the clot-busting medications and stents available today. So the doctors observed him. That evening, he developed crushing chest pain, caused by a massive myocardial infarction of the anterior (front) wall of the heart. The only treatment available was morphine and oxygen-comfort care-while the most important part of his heart muscle died. His cardiologist later told my mom he would likely die within five years. That hospital later started trials of streptokinase, a medication that would have dissolved the clot that caused the heart attack.

At the age of 57, my dad developed "indigestion," for which he started taking antacids. One evening he developed more severe indigestion and collapsed right in front of my mom. Paramedics performed CPR, but he had already passed. I received the news while in residency, working in the emergency room; taking care of other patients with chest pain. This traumatic event has shaped me in many ways, not the least of which is to take all chest pain very seriously. I have learned to appreciate how precious life is and to cherish every day.

Robert Ziltzer, MD
@robziltzerMD

We discovered years ago, coincidentally, that Rob Ziltzer and I have a similar beginning in medicine, initiated by our fathers' early heart attacks. While growing up in Chicagoland as a child, I always wanted to be a physician. When it became time to actually go to college and choose a major of study, I did not start as a pre-med student but as an engineering student. At the beginning of the first winter break of college, my father entered the hospital at the age of 52 with a heart attack. He spent 11 days in the hospital, a length of stay that now frequently lasts only 24 hours. As I was home on vacation during this time, I was able to visit him every day and see the great life-saving medical care he received. This event moved me and inspired me to rethink my career path, change direction, and go into pre-med studies. From that moment, I have been interested in improving health, especially in preventing heart attacks and other metabolic diseases.

Writing a book, as well as running a successful medical weight loss practice, is not accomplished alone. I want to first thank Rob Ziltzer for being the one who first hired me out of medical residency and the one whom I bounce ideas off and have (physically) shared an office with every single workday since 2001. It has been an ongoing medical and business consultation for 17 years.

I want to thank the staff and physicians of Scottsdale Weight Loss Center for making it a wonderful place to work, as well as so expertly and caringly providing 5-Star medical care to our patients.

I want to thank the Obesity Medicine Association (OMA), a society of over 2300 clinicians dedicated to the treatment of obesity, for fulfilling me professionally since 2005 and equipping me with the tools to actually make a career out of obesity medicine. I am proud to share that beginning in September 2019, I will give back to the field of Obesity Medicine by serving a 2-year term as the president of the OMA.

I want to thank my family: Jordan and Judi Primack; my parents, who successfully raised 3 boys (2 attorneys and 1 doctor—pretty good, right?) and my kids, Sam, Lauren, and Aidan, who make me proud to be your parent every day and give me a reason to wake up in the morning and come home in the evening

Last and certainly not at all least, I want to thank my patients, the several thousand unique individuals who have trusted me to serve as their physician, sharing with me the intricacies of their daily lives, their struggles with weight, as well as the joys (often for the first time) in their success at weight loss and weight maintenance.

Craig Primack, MD
www.doctorprimack.com
@DoctorPrimack

Letter to Our Reader

Dear Reader:

We guess that you are like the patients we've seen over the years.

You are frustrated, tired, discouraged, hungry, and burned out. You are at your highest weight ever, and you no longer recognize or even like yourself in photos.

You have probably tried diet after diet and still have been unable to get control of your weight. You've been chasing diets, and you're losing the race. In fact, in a survey of our patients, we've found that many have tried ten or more diets with no results; some have tried hundreds.

Your clothes are tight, and you feel lethargic. Every seat seems too small, and seatbelts are too short. You can't engage in the activities that once brought you joy: playing with your children or grandchildren; hiking; traveling, or even simple things, like crossing your legs or sitting on the floor.

We know these things because we have seen them before in our patients.

"I have struggled with weight since having my kids. My weight has been up and down for years. I have tried several diets both self-driven and other major plans."

"I have probably been on over 50 diets in my life, and if I were to add all the weight I've gained and lost and gained, it would be well over 1000 pounds."

"I have been struggling with my weight for 25 years and have tried every diet out there with marginal success and ultimate failure, always gaining all my weight back each time."

You long for a thinner, healthier, more energetic, and happier life.

If this is where you are, you are reading the right book. We want to give you hope for a different life. A life in which you are in control, in which you look and feel great, and one in which your weight isn't the central focus of your life.

We are excited to share the ideas in this book because we can help you achieve your goals. We've already helped thousands of people like you take control of their lives.

Why is weight loss so easy for some and seemingly impossible for others?

You probably know friends, family members, or spouses who have quickly and easily shed a few extra pounds by following a self-help diet or the next fad or *du jour* diet. You may have a spouse who gave up regular sodas for a month and lost 10 pounds. Or you have friends who swear by a program that worked for them, but the same diet left you feeling hungry and cranky. "Why is weight loss so hard for me?" you may be asking.

While we like to think we live in a "one-size-fits-all" world, the truth is that weight loss is a complex and highly individualized issue.

The weight loss problem is complex. It is not just a matter of eating less and exercising more (as some would suggest); it is, rather, an interplay of nutrition, psychology, body chemistry, physical exercise, and genetic factors.

You can't achieve weight loss by not eating. While smokers may stop smoking, people fighting obesity can't stop eating, so the solution is more complicated.

Losing weight and maintaining a healthy weight are two entirely different strategies. Some individuals may be able to follow a diet and lose the weight but are unable to keep that weight off after weight loss is achieved. Some people find weight maintenance more difficult than losing weight.

Losing weight is hard if not impossible, so why will your program work for me?

Think about it: When you have a severe or pervasive problem in other areas of your life, you generally go to an expert.

If you have been trying to invest on your own and have not been able to generate wealth, chances are that you will hire an expert: a stockbroker or investment advisor.

If you have a termite-infestation in your home, the chances are that you will not opt for the do-it-yourself kit from your hardware store. Instead, you will hire an expert: an exterminator.

In fact, for serious health issues like cancer, you would likely never consider treating yourself or reading an article on the internet on how to do chemotherapy; instead, you would be more likely to treat your cancer by consulting a trusted professional who is highly skilled, trained, and educated on state-of-the-art medical issues. You will look for and receive care from an expert: an oncologist (cancer physician).

Therefore, when your health is at risk because of serious weight issues, why would you trust your solution to anyone except an expert: an obesity medicine specialist?

Medical issues need medical solutions, and when you need serious, significant weight loss, you need solutions prescribed by physicians with expertise in weight loss!

The reason we have been successful in our practice is that we uniquely understand the interplay of the complex issues that impact hunger, energy, nutrition, and metabolism. We can prescribe a unique and tailored approach that works for the individual.

And while we'll share the details of our experiences and training in the About the Authors section, let us highlight just a few of our credentials below:

- Voted one of *PHOENIX Magazine*'s Top Docs 12 times
- Diplomates of the American Board of Obesity Medicine, the organization that certifies expertise in weight management.
- Nationally recognized as experts and speakers in obesity medicine

- Serves on the board of the Obesity Medicine Association, and elected president-elect of the society in fall of 2017.
- Appearances on national and local TV shows, including *The Dr. Oz Show*, as an expert on weight loss topics.
- Our patients have lost combined nearly a quarter of a million pounds, including actors, celebrities, and professional athletes.

In this book, we'll share with you some of the complex issues that impact your ability to lose weight, and we'll help you see why a personalized medical approach is the solution you have been looking for.

Throughout our discussion, we'll share some of our many success stories with individuals just like you who have struggled with their weight. We'll share their struggles and the solutions we crafted that made these individuals finally able to realize their goals.

We'll go into detail about patients like Yolanda who lost 45 pounds, Diane who lost 26 pounds, Ellen who lost 65 pounds, Janet who lost 86 pounds, and Danny who lost 106 pounds. We'll share story after story detailing the successes we've had in working with individuals who never thought they would have their weight under control. Better yet, we'll share even more details of how these patients have not only lost the weight but also kept it off.

Are you ready to be inspired? Are you prepared to regain hope for a different life?

We invite you to read on and learn how you, too, can take control of your weight and your life.

Robert Ziltzer, MD
Craig Primack, MD

Foreword

Everything we all think we know about weight loss is false.

This book does a great job of dispelling the myths about weight loss and teaching current science. Obesity was recognized in America as a disease in 2013 by the American Medical Association. This recognition means that obesity should be treated by a health care provider in a serious fashion, similar to heart disease or diabetes.

Thinking we can just "Eat Less, Exercise More" is an overused, antiquated concept that blames the individual for developing the disease of obesity. We know that obesity is 40-70% caused by genetic factors outside of an individual's control. 85-90% of people who do the "Eat Less, Move More" approach quickly regain any lost weight, not due to a lack of willpower, but due to the body's ability to protect itself.

Regardless of whether a person is heavy or not, when the body loses weight, it fights to regain any lost pounds through both hormonal and metabolic mechanisms. The body is very, very good at protecting itself. We call this body weight regulation.

After weight loss, the body does not accept the new, lower weight as "normal." It does not reset the weight set-point. It does not restore metabolism.

That's why this book is important. It focuses on obesity as a chronic disease, and it reviews the evidence-based treatment options that have been shown to be helpful long-term. It reviews the importance of having a healthcare provider leading the team, and the importance of a multi-component approach that includes medical supervision, healthy eating, physical activity, and intensive lifestyle education.

Don't go at it alone. By working with a team of trained healthcare professionals, your odds at beating this are improved exponentially.

Ethan Lazarus, MD, FOMA

Table of Contents

Introduction 1

Chapter 1: Obesity is a Disease 7

Chapter 2: Developing a Comprehensive Weight Loss Program: A Four-Legged Approach..................... 27

Chapter 3: The First Leg: Medical Management 39

Chapter 4: The Second Leg: Nutrition 67

Chapter 5: The Third Leg: Activity 93

Chapter 6: The Fourth Leg: Education 107

Chapter 7: Your Weight Loss Journey with Weight Loss Centers 127

Chapter 8: Maintenance and Beyond: How to Keep It Off! 149

Chapter 9: Success! 157

Suggested Reading 177

Reference Notes 179

About the Authors 183

Chasing Diets

Stop the Endless Search and Discover the Solution

Introduction

AS TWO PHYSICIANS who became board certified in internal medicine and pediatrics, we spent the first half of our careers treating conditions such as diabetes, high blood pressure, arthritis, chronic obstructive pulmonary disease, and many conditions for which the current treatment is medication. That is what medical school taught us. If someone's blood pressure is high, you put them on a pill. If someone's cholesterol is high, you put them on another pill. "Mr. Jones, your blood pressure is high. Here's a medication to bring your blood pressure down. I'll see you back next week." We would often see patients who were on a dozen medications for which obesity was the underlying cause of those diseases. However, in the current sad state of the insurance world, all the monetary incentives in our health care system promote the use of medications as the quickest and most natural thing for physicians to do. Intensive counseling takes lots of time.

We knew there had to be a better way. In fact, when we began practice, we semi-jokingly said, "If we can help patients lose a lot of weight and keep it off, we will leave primary care practice and go into full-time weight-loss medicine, where we can take patients off all those medicines."

As it turns out, successful weight loss is not a joke. It *is* possible, and with the right personalized weight loss plan, it is even *probable* that you can lose weight and keep it off, as long as you get professional help.

As a result (and after years of learning and practice on our part), we gained advanced knowledge and state-of-the-art tools that we have now brought into practice to help patients lose weight. Remember, we spent the first half of our careers putting patients on medications for all these weight-related conditions, and we happily continue to spend the second half of our careers taking people off most of those medications.

We live in a world in which there are tens of thousands of books on diets. Amazon lists over 60,000 diet books. It seems that every month a new diet book comes out with the promise that *this* will be the ultimate solution or the latest trick or secret to the obesity crisis. Too often we read newspaper articles or magazine articles touting the next great diet. Even top TV hosts come out with more fad diets, episode after episode. When you get tired of these trends, there are numerous ads for quick-fix workouts and untested, unproven supplements looking to consume your hard-earned dollars.

What you have learned and experienced, up until now, has likely shown you that none of these non-medical diets, workouts, or supplements work. If they did, we would write the diet book, sell the online workout or special supplement, and you would buy them, ending America's obesity epidemic.

Unfortunately, that will not happen. When you Google the word "obesity," you will see that obesity is considered a self-treatable condition. In reality, nothing could be further from the truth. **Obesity is a serious and chronic medical disease that requires treatment by a physician or other healthcare provider. It is time for a new conversation about the way society thinks about obesity. It is time for a new paradigm. Only then will the obesity epidemic improve.**

In this book, we will explain why this is true.

Fortunately, we discovered that with the right tools, patients can be successful both in losing and keeping weight off, so we decided to stop practicing primary care. We went into this career in 2006 to change lives.

We see people who were once unable to walk one block regain their health, get off medications, and even achieve physical feats that they never thought possible. For example, we have had patients run 5Ks and marathons, hike to the bottom of the Grand Canyon and back, and even become triathletes when before, they could not have imagined walking even a mile.

The truth is, we believe in you before you believe in yourself; it is time for you to believe. While there are no do-it-yourself magic diets or herbal supplements, dramatic success is likely.

An excellent personalized weight loss plan takes into account science, persistence, and an overall comprehensive approach. You will not wake up tomorrow and find that there is a brand new "fad" diet that has proven to be better than a personalized, comprehensive weight loss plan.

Let's look at Joyce's story. Joyce suffered a shoulder fracture and was not able to exercise for fear of falling. Joyce reported, "My body atrophied, and I gained weight … A LOT of weight. I felt like my body had been taken over by an imposter that I did not even recognize in the mirror, and I was SO TIRED all the time." She lost some of the weight on her own, but it took 3 ½ years. Then her doctor referred Joyce to us. "In just two months I lost twenty pounds and got back to my weight before breaking my shoulder ... And this is while traveling and vacationing! Then, I continued to lose another twenty pounds back to my weight when I met my husband twenty-five years ago! And it was easy. I feel like myself again. I have gone from a size 18 to a size 10, and my energy level is back ... Ask my friends. I feel like doing fun things again." Joyce found that with the right kind of medical care, losing the weight was faster and easier than on her own.

We are going to help make this process a lot easier for you as we have done for thousands of patients like Joyce. When you choose a comprehensive medical weight loss program, it will be evident that things will be different from your do-it-yourself diet. After visiting with your weight-loss physician the first time; undergoing a thorough history, physical exam, and lab tests, he will start you on a comprehensive plan which includes diet, exercise, a series of targeted lifestyle education classes, and possibly weight loss medications. This combination of treatment is the way to lose the greatest amount of weight in the shortest amount of time and with the least amount of hunger.

We believe you can lose your excess weight and keep it off.

Now *you* have to believe in *you*.

Chapter 1: Obesity is a Disease

THROUGHOUT THIS BOOK, we will follow Danny and his wife, Margaret. In many ways, Danny was like so many of our patients. He was heavy growing up through middle school and high school. Then in college Danny was able to adopt a healthier and more active lifestyle and was able to control his weight.

"In my twenties, things changed, and I began drinking more sugary beverages and developed some poor eating habits. When I went to see a doctor about my gradual weight gain, I was able to lose some of that weight by giving up my 'Big Gulps,' eating more chicken and lean proteins and less pizza and chips. I combined this with playing more basketball and racquetball and being more active.

"But things changed over time, and I slowly gained ten pounds, 15 pounds, and 20 pounds as I fell back into

poor habits. Each time I found a new weight loss scheme (like the infamous cabbage soup diet as well as other diets du jour) I lost a few pounds. But eventually I gained back even more than I lost.

"I was not sleeping well. My wife Margaret expressed concern about my snoring. At times, she worried that long pauses between my heavy snoring might mean I might not wake up the next day. She wanted me to see a doctor for my health, and partly so that she could get a good night's sleep. At times she had to sleep in another room to get back to sleep.

"As I approached my 50th birthday, I weighed nearly 270 pounds and was becoming more frustrated and ashamed. I remember the embarrassment of being at a Phoenix Suns game. I was there with my son and sitting next to us was another gentleman and his child. It was the two dads sitting next to each other. I didn't know this guy, and our sons were sitting kind of on the outside of us. I remember he was visibly getting frustrated or annoyed, and not really saying anything. He was giving me looks and overreacting physically to show his displeasure or annoyance. I don't remember the exact words that he used, but something to the effect of, 'Hey, would you mind? You keep banging into me.' It wasn't in a nice way like, 'Hey, excuse me, can you please try not to do this?' His frustrations were clearly coming out. In the back of my mind, I empathized with what he was

feeling, but I was insulted and embarrassed at the same time. I understood why the man felt that way. I apologized, but it was so embarrassing with my son witnessing the entire event.

"I remember thinking that I wished that others could understand that my weight issues were something that I struggled with and not a conscious choice."

Does this sound familiar to you? Then read on. There is hope.

Obesity is a serious and chronic disease, which is defined as having excess body fat. Being overweight or obese is measured along a continuum, usually by using Body Mass Index (BMI).

What is obesity?

How does someone know if he or she is at a healthy weight, overweight or has obesity? This question is surprisingly difficult to answer since most single measures of body fat are imperfect. Let us explore how we assess an individual's body fat.

Body Mass Index (BMI) is calculated by dividing weight in pounds by height in inches squared and then multiplying by a conversion factor of 703. For example, a person who is 5'4" (64 inches) and weighs 140 pounds has a BMI of 24 (140 / 4096 then multiplied by 703 =

24). A person who is 6'2" (74 inches) and weighs 210 pounds has a BMI of 27 (210 / 5476 then multiplied by 703 = 27). Fortunately, calculating your BMI is easy. You can input your weight in one of the many online calculators.

Your BMI score will, in part, determine whether your weight is defined as normal, overweight, obese, or severely obese.

To determine your BMI, visit ChasingDiets.com

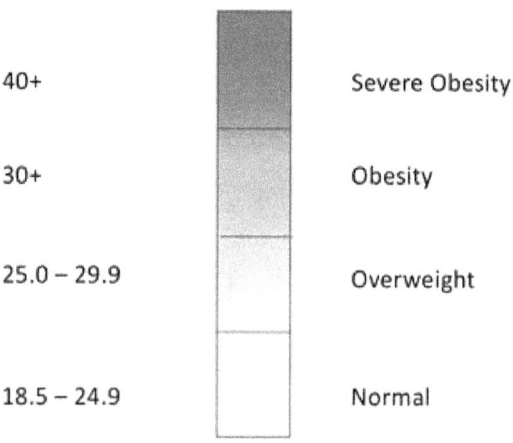

As BMI goes up, the risk for other closely related medical conditions, in addition to obesity, correspondingly increases.

However, **BMI scores alone are an imperfect measure.** For example, there are some very muscular athletes with a very high BMI who do not have obesity. Likewise, there may be a 60-year-old woman with a BMI of 24 but whose body fat is 44% (over 32% is considered obesity). This discrepancy is usually due to a condition characterized by loss of muscle mass, called sarcopenia. That person may still suffer from all the health consequences of obesity.

Another measure to determine excess body fat is to calculate waist size. By measuring around the belly (on a line even with the belly-button), women with a waist size greater than 35" and men with a waist size greater than 40" likely have excess body fat.

Other measures include hydrostatic weighing (water displacement), Bod Pods® (calculating air displacement), DEXA scans and medical scales (bioelectric impedance); each of these methods can also provide a picture of body fat. Bioelectric impedance sends a tiny electric current across the body, and measures how much reaches the other side. Fat is an insulator, and water and muscle are conductors. Excess body fat will reduce the amount of electricity that crosses the body. The scale translates this number to a body fat percentage. Bioelectric impedance has the advantage of being quick, accurate, and reproducible. As a result, we recommend a combination of BMI measurement, waist size, and bioelectric impedance.

> *Because none of these measures are perfect, combining several methods will identify most people with excess body fat who may need treatment. It requires a medical professional to make a proper diagnosis and treatment plan.*

Is obesity a medical disease?

Yes! In 2013, the American Medical Association declared that **obesity is a chronic medical disease.** Chronic means it cannot be cured. This announcement was a significant landmark in medicine and in weight loss treatment. Weight loss is no longer a condition of poor self-control, laziness, or lack of motivation. No one chooses to be overweight, just as no one chooses to have cancer, diabetes, high blood pressure, or high cholesterol.

A *disease*, as defined by Merriam-Webster, is *"a condition of the living animal or plant body or one of its parts that impairs normal functioning and is typically manifested by distinguishing signs and symptoms.* Obesity impairs normal function in almost every organ by causing diabetes, heart disease, fatty liver disease, cancer, arthritis, lumbar disc disease, sleep apnea, edema, and increased pressure on the brain. Obesity has both signs that can be measured (BMI) and symptoms that can be felt by the patient, such as shortness of breath or back pain. The greater one's excess body fat, the more likely he or she is to experience symptoms and develop the body function changes above.

> *Obesity is a chronic medical disease, and, like hypertension, can be treated by physicians.*

Let's explore more reasons why we absolutely believe (as does the AMA) that obesity is a disease; not only a disease but also a serious and chronic disease.

If ideal weight was merely a choice, we would not have so many overweight people. Very simply, if diet and exercise worked on their own, we would not have almost 100 million people in the United States who suffer with obesity.

Next, losing weight often leads to weight regain. Weight loss causes long-term changes in the hormones that increase hunger and reduce metabolism. These physiological changes persist until we return to our baseline (lifetime highest) weight. There is no way to undo these changes, but we do have very successful long-term treatment plans. This book is all about successful treatment plans. We manage the lower metabolism by increasing exercise, and we manage hunger by introducing frequent small meals and weight loss medications. This treatment method is far from simple, self-help dieting.

The only effective and long-term solution for obesity is prolonged treatment under the care of a trained physician. Treatment will include a comprehensive and personalized plan, and over time, it can be modified to your needs. It does not mean you will need to be on medication or a highly restricted diet indefinitely, but you will need some ongoing treatment.

Obesity is also a disease because our fat itself can be sick. There are microscopic changes within fat cells that occur when they grow too large. You may have heard terms like cardiomyopathy, which means a sick heart or nephropathy, which means sick kidneys. The name for sick fat cells is called **adiposopathy**. Think of each fat cell as a balloon, which is continually inflated. When the fat cells become enlarged, the cells start sending out inflammatory signals (such as interleukins and tumor necrosis factor). Those hormonal signals travel through the blood to other parts of the body, signaling "danger/inflammation" with a resultant increase in blood pressure, blood sugar, and swelling of the artery lining. They also cause many other metabolic problems that go along with being overweight.

A person who is overweight or has obesity can be treated but not cured. We can put the disease in remission, but we cannot cure it. The condition persists, even if you have lost all of your excess weight, and it will take long-term treatment to keep it controlled. When you lose weight, leptin levels reduce (you will learn about these hormones later), and as a result, you will be less satiated (full), and your metabolism will be lower than it was before.

Additionally, the hunger hormone (ghrelin) will increase. As a result, your body will always strive to get back to your lifetime highest weight. So losing weight is a way of getting your obesity "in control," just like taking blood pressure or diabetes medication controls those diseases.

What is the physiology of obesity?

Losing and then maintaining weight after weight loss is challenging because of the body's response to calorie restriction. As you lose weight, your metabolism slows down. The human race started as hunters, gatherers, and then farmers. During times of famine, our metabolism had to slow down, and hunger had to be turned up to keep us alive and reproducing. The **hypothalamus**, a portion the size of a blueberry in the center of the brain, controls many of these body functions. There are sensors from around the body that communicate with the hypothalamus through special proteins called hormones. Areas of the body act as sensory organs sending these hormonal signals to the brain from the small intestine, stomach, pancreas, biliary tract and fat itself. These hormones are proteins that travel through the blood to the hypothalamus and signal whether one should be hungry or full; therefore, whether to eat or not to eat.

As we lose weight, these hormones change, increasing hunger, lowering feelings of fullness (satiety), and severely decreasing our metabolism. Such changes make losing weight and maintaining that loss on your own very difficult.

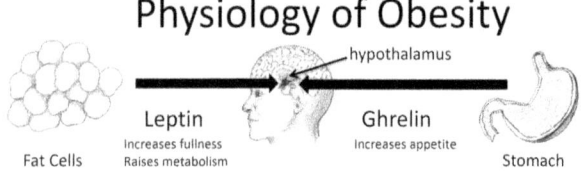

After weight loss: ⬇ Leptin and ⬆ Ghrelin, causing weight regain.

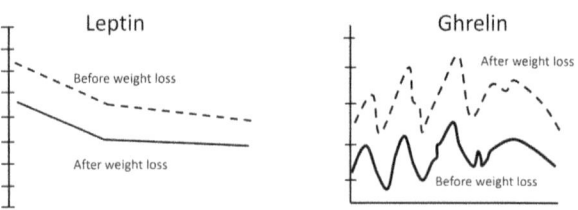

Figure 1. The physiology of obesity. Note that leptin secreted by fat cells increases satiety and increases

metabolism, and ghrelin secreted by the stomach, increases appetite. Ghrelin levels drop after eating and rise before meals. After weight loss, leptin levels decrease and remain decreased, and ghrelin rises and stays that way.

What is the role of hormones in metabolism and appetite?

You may have heard, "Just stop eating when you are full." If it were that easy, don't you think we would all be doing it? Did you stop to think that maybe, just maybe, people with obesity do not feel the same levels of fullness and hunger than others?

Leptin is a hormone made in your fat cells (adipose tissue) that has two main functions. First, it raises your metabolism; and secondly, it increases satiety, the sensation of fullness. As you gain weight and as your fat cells expand, your body makes more leptin, causing a lowering of appetite and a rising of metabolism. When people lose weight, leptin levels go down because fat cells produce less. As a result, metabolism and satiety decrease. We know that people who have gone below their lifetime highest weight have lower leptin levels, and ***those levels may never return to normal*** (sometimes even if they regain their weight).

An important byproduct of weight gain is **leptin resistance**. The problem is that as people gain weight, their body becomes resistant to leptin. In leptin resistance, even though the body has a lot of leptin circulating, it doesn't seem to work as well. As they lose weight, they become more sensitive to their leptin. It is for this reason that leptin injections are ineffective in weight loss. One possible future treatment for obesity may be the injection of forms of leptin in combination with other medications that counteract leptin resistance or even the use of leptin to help with weight loss maintenance.

The second main hormone is **ghrelin**. Ghrelin is made mostly in the lining of the greater curvature (lower part) of the stomach and also circulates through the blood. Like leptin, it enters the hypothalamus but instead, signals hunger. Ghrelin elevates before each meal and decreases when we eat. Moreover, ghrelin levels rise in the evening. It is for this reason that many individuals struggle with hunger at night. Ghrelin decreases while we sleep, so getting to sleep before the nighttime ghrelin surge helps reduce daily food intake. When people lose weight, their baseline and peak ghrelin levels rise, and those levels remain at those highs as long as they stay below their lifetime highest weight. This increase in ghrelin probably lasts for the rest of their lives. **It is primarily, but not exclusively these two important hormones that create the ongoing battle of rising appetite and lowering metabolism for dieters**.

Are there other physiological factors in weight loss?

The thyroid gland also plays a role in slowing weight regain. There are two primary forms of thyroid hormone—T3 (the more active hormone) and T4 (the less active and storage form)—that control functions of the body, including metabolism. These hormones increase metabolism, including body temperature and growth. People with low levels of thyroid hormone have low body temperature, feel cold, have low energy, gain weight, have constipation, and experience hair loss.

T3 is a potent thyroid hormone, which rapidly raises metabolism. As we lose weight, T3 levels are lowered resulting in what has been called the "famine response." This slowing of the metabolism happens during prolonged dieting, as the body converts some T3 to a less active form, called reverse T3. Also, the usual thyroid test (thyroid stimulating hormone or TSH for short), is often normal despite low thyroid levels. The famine response causes one to stop losing weight despite very low food intake.

Insulin is another important hormone that controls weight, and its job is to help drive sugar from the bloodstream into our cells. Insulin is the key that opens the door, allowing sugar into the muscles, fat cells, and most organs. Sugar and starch (after being broken down to simple sugar) travels through the intestines where it is absorbed into the bloodstream. The presence of increased sugar in the blood signals our pancreas to release insulin. When sugar levels remain high in the bloodstream, they cause damage to many organs of our body. So to protect the body and store the energy for later use, our body will work to get that sugar out of the bloodstream. As a result, the pancreas continues to secrete insulin, and that drives sugar into the fat cells where it is processed into additional fat. Insulin is the primary driver of fat building. The more insulin we make, the more fat we produce. It is for this reason that high carbohydrate diets often lead to weight gain.

Finally, the hormone **cortisol** also plays a role in weight gain. Cortisol is a stress hormone made in our adrenal glands. We have two adrenal glands, one on each side of our body, just above each kidney. Cortisol is required to live and respond to acute and chronic stresses to our body. A high level of cortisol causes weight gain from several mechanisms. First, cortisol raises blood sugar, which, in turn, increases insulin (which builds fat). Second, when we become stressed or when we reduce our sleep (another stressor), cortisol levels rise causing us to increase sugar and deposit fat in the center of our bodies along the midline, especially in the abdomen, waist, and thigh area. If you have ever seen someone prescribed high doses of corticosteroids such as prednisone, you will notice that their bellies are protuberant, and at the same time their arms and legs are skinny; that is the effect of cortisol.

What have we learned from studies of self-dieters who lose significant amounts of weight?

This physiology of obesity was documented quite well in *The Biggest Loser* study. This study followed fourteen individuals from season eight of *The Biggest Loser* television show for six years. The study, which looked at the metabolism of the contestants, showed that they lost an average of 128 pounds each by the end of the competition. Six years later each contestant regained an average of 90 pounds. Also, their metabolism was 500 calories per day lower than expected (compared to people who have never gained weight). In other words, they were miserable on the paltry amount of food required for weight maintenance.

This study may cause one to feel that weight loss is futile, but that is not the case. This book is about taking all we have learned from studies such as *Biggest Loser*, our training, and decades of experience to give you the tools to prevent the weight regain that *The Biggest Loser* contestants experienced.

What are the similarities between hypertension and obesity?

Obesity is a disease akin to hypertension or high blood pressure. Hypertension is a disorder in which factors within the body create a higher blood pressure set point. Normal blood pressure is less than 120 (systolic, the top number) over 80 (diastolic, the bottom number). An example of abnormal blood pressure is 160/96. After diagnosis, physicians start treatment by recommending a low salt diet and exercise. Alone, this rarely reduces a patient's blood pressure. They also advise losing weight, usually without any specific recommendation of how to do this. Those attempts typically fail. If blood pressure remains untreated for months to years, the pressure on the artery walls causes them to harden and narrow, developing cholesterol plaques, which ultimately cause artery blockage. The results of artery narrowing and blockage are strokes and heart attacks. The increased pressure also hammers at the kidneys and causes them to fail. It also causes increased strain on the heart muscle, with either thickening and stiffness or weakness, enlargement, and heart failure.

Fortunately, for blood pressure, there are more than one hundred choices of **anti-hypertensive medications** (in contrast to weight loss medications, in which there are only seven to ten). As long as you continue to take drugs, your blood pressure (or your diabetes) will likely remain under good control. If you stop the medication, your blood pressure will increase. These medicines do not cure blood pressure problems; they only treat and control it. Once begun, the only hope of eliminating the lifelong need for blood pressure pills is through weight loss.

Can you lose weight on your own? "Sylvia's Story"

At 220 pounds, Sylvia came to us having given up nearly all hope of losing weight. She had gone from one diet to another, including Atkins®, South Beach®, Weight Watchers®, and Nutrisystem®. She lost only five to ten pounds on nearly all of her attempts, following them for only as long as three weeks and regaining all of her weight within a few months. On her most recent attempt at Atkins, she was able to lose 30 pounds. This time she was very motivated, as her daughter's wedding was soon approaching. While she described the diet as stressful and challenging to follow, she kept her focus on fitting into her dress and posing for pictures. As soon as the wedding was over, she started to regain, and within eight months returned to her baseline highest weight. This story is typical in that a significant goal such as a family event, high school reunion, or threat of having to take new blood pressure or cholesterol medication can lead to a short-term loss. Rarely can people sustain the diet long enough to get to their real goal, and those few who can almost never keep the pounds off.

The truth is that most people will try to lose weight on their own, and very few will be successful. At the very best, they may lose a few pounds only to regain it. They spend their entire lives dieting, losing and gaining, and losing and regaining. At the end of the day they have not achieved anything, and they certainly have not lost any weight.

By the time patients finally decide that they need to see a physician to lose weight, they have tried an average of eight to twelve diets. We ask all of our patients, "How many diets have you been on?" We have heard answers like "50 diets," "100 diets," "too many to count," "I've tried every one of them," and an "infinite" number of diets.

Won't trying just one more make you successful this time?

Unfortunately, no.

The truth is that losing weight on your own is a no-win venture. Only five percent of people who attempt their own diets can lose weight and maintain it.

The answer to the question, "Can I lose weight on my own?" is both yes and no. You can lose weight short-term, but you can't keep it off for long. We've had some patients who can lose weight on their own; some of them have lost weight every time they've dieted, but after a while, they can't keep it off. So the better question is not, "Can I lose weight on my own?" but, "Can I keep it off?"

John saw his family physician for his annual checkup. His doctor was concerned that his blood sugar was in the prediabetes range, and his blood pressure was 145/96, a level of hypertension that could, over time, lead to stroke and heart disease. He had gained eight pounds since his physical a year ago and was now up to 247 pounds. His physician advised a blood pressure medication and metformin to reduce his blood sugar. On his own, he sought the help of an obesity medicine physician in hopes that he could get off these medications. His physician had previously advised he "go on a diet" and begin exercising, and didn't give him any specific advice except to "watch what you are eating." But none of these efforts had worked for him. He was only able to stay on each diet for two days before caving to his nighttime cravings. He felt more feelings of shame and failure with each diet.

Then John came to our practice. He began a diet consisting of medical meal replacements and Contrave®, a weight loss medication that helped reduce the cravings he had for sweets at night. He was skeptical that he could lose much weight, so he set a modest goal to lose 20 pounds. When he reached 220 pounds (27 pounds of weight loss), his blood pressure dropped dramatically, and he was able to stop his blood pressure medication. His blood pressure was lower than it was before he started losing weight (when he was on a blood pressure medication). He set a goal to reach 200 pounds. When he reached that milestone, he set a new goal of 190 pounds. Now at 181 pounds, he is off all blood sugar and blood pressure pills and wonders why anyone would need to take such medication when he or she could just lose weight. John expressed frustration that his primary care physician had not referred him to a specialist for weight loss, but instead had given him the same advice most doctors do: "Eat less and exercise more." For John, obesity was the cause of both medical problems, and losing weight brought both of them under control. We say that he is in control but not cured. He will always need to have a maintenance plan to preserve his weight loss to remain off of his blood pressure and diabetes medications.

Chapter 2: Developing a Comprehensive Weight Loss Program: A Four-Legged Approach

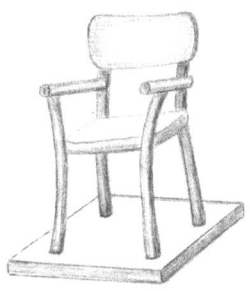

DANNY: "ONCE UPON a time, there was a boy who became an overweight adult. He went to school, worked hard, met his wife, had children and became a man with obesity. The weight gain started at a young age, and over time defined him. [Through a comprehensive medical weight loss program] he discovered nutrition, exercise, knowledge and better health on his journey. He lost weight, over 100 pounds—and body fat–down 25 percent. He

rediscovered life and led over a dozen friends down the same path.

"I am Danny P, the man with obesity that learned nutrition and exercise are key to a healthy and longer life. My accomplishments have been both big and small, physical and emotional. I have developed new eating habits and discovered it is fun to exercise! My mantra has changed from 'live to eat' to 'eat to live'!

"In addition to losing weight, body fat, and inches, I also significantly lowered my blood pressure and took control of and accountability for my health. I have benefited from my accomplishments in ways that I had not considered—buying clothes off the rack at regular stores, comfortably sitting (and fitting) in my assigned seat on airplanes and sporting events, participating more fully in sports and other activities (versus making excuses), sleeping better, and waking up energized and ready to face the day."

Danny was successful because he utilized a comprehensive approach to weight loss. His treatment plan included a low carb, very low-calorie medical diet, behavior education classes, weekly visits for accountability and guidance, and regular walking. Now over one year into maintenance, he has kept off 106 pounds!

There are four critical components of any comprehensive weight loss program, and each of these four components is essential to a successful program. **Lose one of the elements, and you are more likely to fail to lose the weight and even less likely to keep it off.**

The first and most essential (and most often missing) component is medical management, which includes both accountability and medications. Some people refer to drugs used for the treatment of obesity as appetite suppressants or anti-obesity medications. We will refer to them as *weight loss medications*. We will discuss specific medications later on in this book. Part of medical management also includes reducing medicines that you may already be on which cause weight gain. As you work with a physician as part of your weight loss program, he or she can speak with your primary doctor or specialist who put you on the medicine in the first place. Often there are equivalent alternatives that are less likely to cause weight gain. For example, many antidepressants cause weight gain and when changed, make losing weight a lot easier.

Second is a nutritional or dietary change. A meal plan best suited to each person leading to calorie reduction while providing complete nutrition is the foundation of any weight loss plan. See the chapter "Which Diet is Best" for a full discussion of the diet options.

The third is an activity plan. Exercise is a small part of weight loss but a critical part of weight maintenance. It is the activity plan that allows you to eat more in maintenance without having to restrict food intake severely. One of the most common mistakes that we see occurs on each January 1st when millions of people flock to gyms to work out in the hope of losing weight. They start exercising and expect that the pounds will drop off. Unfortunately, this almost never works, and there are several reasons for this. The first is when you exercise too much, you tend to be hungrier and tend to overeat. The second relates to your body's response to exercise.

We used to tell people that if you wanted to burn a pound of fat, you'd have to burn 3,500 calories. Studies now show that you need to burn between 4,500 and 7,000 for each pound of fat.

Let's translate that to running. If you had magic legs and used running as your weight loss tool, let's see how much running you'd have to do to burn two pounds of fat per week.

Since one pound of fat contains 4,500 calories and each mile burns 100 calories, you would have to run 90 miles to burn two pounds of fat. Try doing that without increasing your calorie intake. As a result, it is virtually impossible to lose weight exclusively through exercise. In truth, 80% to 90% of weight loss relates to nutritional intake and adequate sleep, and only 10–20% of your weight loss is related to exercise.

What is the role of exercise in your weight loss plan? In our experience, exercise is the key to keeping off weight. The National Weight Control Registry, an extensive database of people who have maintained at least 30 pounds of weight loss for a year, has shown that the average successful participant burns around 2,500 exercise calories per week. How much exercise is that? It equates to approximately 10,000 steps of walking per day or five hours per week of cardiovascular exercise or weight training. **Again, you should think of dieting and limiting food intake as being the key to losing weight, while making sure you add adequate sleep. Exercise is the key to keeping off weight.**

The fourth component is education, often delivered in a series of classes that include self-monitoring, learning how to manage triggers that make you want to eat, planning for social meals, and practicing mindfulness. Sometimes these classes are also called lifestyle education. You should start to think of these classes as tools in your weight loss toolbox. You may learn something today that you do not need right now, but you tuck that information away in your toolbox.

Somewhere down the line, you will face a situation in which the information will be useful. It is at that point you will pull it out of your toolbox and use it. When you learn from challenging situations, the next time you are in the same situation, you will be more prepared to manage that challenge.

Weight will vary during maintenance, up and down a few pounds, quite often. Education helps us learn to self-monitor and avoid triggers and situations that lead to more significant weight gain.

Does the plan need all four parts to work?

As mentioned previously, there are four components of a successful weight loss program. **Any time you omit any one of these four components your plan is more likely to fail.** Think of it as four legs of a chair. Remove one leg, and you will have a difficult time maintaining balance on that chair.

Weight loss medications alone will lead to minimal results. Also, dieting without adding exercise may lead to weight loss but rarely long-term success because exercise is such an essential part of weight maintenance. We will discuss further the role of exercise in weight management later in this book. Failure to deal with stress eating, boredom eating, and other lifestyle issues will often lead to weight regain. A successful weight loss program will help you deal with all of the individual components.

We will specifically refer to the components of a behavioral program later in Chapter 6.

To revisit the chair analogy, each component is one leg of the chair. If you solely diet, like many people who start on January 1st or go to the gym, you are balancing on only one leg of the chair. Under stress—and stress always enters our lives at some point—the chair shakes, and you quickly fall over. If you now balance on two legs, such as diet and exercise, you are a little bit better balanced when stress shakes the chair. If you add a third leg (behavior modification) to the chair, your chair is again that much more stable. When you add the fourth component, medical management, you have all four legs of the chair supporting you. Now, when stress comes along and shakes your chair, your strong foundation supports you, and the chances of remaining steady increase.

Using our chair analogy, the final component is the foundation under your "chair": **your maintenance plan.** This is one of the most challenging components since you will battle adverse hormonal changes that guarantee that you will be hungrier and have a lower metabolism than before starting a diet. In our experience, it usually takes 18 months for someone to learn the habits to maintain weight loss. Having expert guidance and coaching through this process to help you navigate the many changes and stresses in your life is critical for long-term maintenance.

Who is the best person to manage my weight loss?

By the time people come to a weight loss physician, they have usually all but given up hope. Many patients have tried what seems like every imaginable diet and plan. It always amazes us that they attempt the same diets over and over again or try every new diet *du jour*. They may lose a few pounds and adhere to a particular diet for one to three weeks, only to be so hungry or bored or restricted that they give up. If they do manage to lose weight, they find that they very quickly regain. A doctor who specializes in or is very knowledgeable about obesity and weight loss should serve as your guide for four main reasons.

Your doctor can find the best diet or nutrition plan for you. A weight loss physician can put you on a personalized diet that gives you all the nutrition you need with far fewer calories, markedly improving the results of the other three aspects of a comprehensive plan.

**Secondly, in medical weight loss programs, you have access to a doctor to prescribe weight loss

medications to treat your weight. The use of weight loss medications rarely leads to weight loss on its own. You should think of weight loss medications as being a helper that allows you to follow your meal plan better, manage hunger, and curb the hormonal drive to overeat.

Third, when you are under the care of a physician, you will obtain guidance for the many challenges that occur in your life, such as vacations, stress eating, boredom eating, and social eating. A weight loss physician will personalize your program for you so that you can be successful. He will coach you through the times when you expect it will be harder to stick to your diet, such as a cruise, a life setback, or holiday parties.

Fourth, a weight loss physician can help design a maintenance plan so that you can maintain the weight that you have lost. Doctors have many tools that you would not have access to on your own.

Medicine is both a science and an art. When you see weight loss physicians, they start with one of the clinically proven weight loss plans that have been shown to work for most people. Each time you visit your physician, he or she will adjust your diet plan to fit your needs best.

In the future, physicians will additionally use genetic testing to assist in choosing the best diet or weight loss medications.

Your weight loss physician is your coach

Your weight loss physician is your weight loss coach. His or her goal is to help you become a successful weight manager rather than a dieter. Professional tennis players like Roger Federer, Rafael Nadal, and the Williams sisters have coaches because they need the insight and accountability that a coach provides.

At the end of the competition, the coach reviews the match, focusing on strengths and weaknesses, and helps guide the player to better performance. The coach ensures that his players are doing their weekly practices and training to maximize their competitive advantage. The coach is there when the player is off his or her game and needs to figure out how to overcome obstacles.

While your weight loss physician isn't monitoring your every move, he or she is there on a regular basis to provide feedback and support. You will come in and see your coach on a regular basis, and if you have had a good week, he or she will likely say, "Great job." If you have had a bad week, he or she (with your help) can discuss strategies to make your next week better.

Your physician coach will help you plan for any circumstances that might present a challenge to the maintenance of your program.

How quickly can I lose weight with a weight loss physician?

One of the greatest advantages of seeing a weight loss physician is the speed of weight loss. The best self-help diets average seven pounds of weight loss in one year. Weight loss under the care of a medical doctor will be much faster than weight loss on your own. For example, in our clinic, patients lose on average 12 to 14 pounds in the first month, 22 pounds in two months, and 33 pounds in three months. Additionally, at one year, our average patient loses 47 pounds (for BMI 40-45). How is this possible? How can someone lose weight and keep it off? **The answer lies in a personalized weight loss plan that incorporates the four elements of a comprehensive weight loss program.**

When someone goes on a crash diet and loses weight quickly, most of what they lose is water and lean body mass-muscle. Crash-dieters often feel terrible and quit. A medical weight loss plan, on the other hand, is nutritionally complete. **That is the essence—providing complete nutrition with fewer calories. Every study on weight loss speed shows that the faster someone**

loses weight in the first month, at two months, three months, the less they will weigh at one year. Faster is better!

Most reputable studies track weight loss for at least a year. Of course, keeping that weight off several years out is the most important. However, one year is a huge landmark. The more aggressive you are in the first few months, the faster your weight loss, and usually the more you will have lost at the end of the year.

Fad diets are an exception to the "faster-is-better" rule. If someone goes on a crash diet and loses a lot of lean body mass, they feel worse the longer they are on their plan. They become malnourished, metabolism drops, and they regain that weight quickly. The key here is to get **complete nutrition on fewer calories**, which is what your physician will help you achieve.

Chapter 3: The First Leg: Medical Management

AT AGE 66, Sue, an RN, decided a year ago her knee arthritis pain was so severe that she scheduled a knee replacement. At an initial weight of 230 pounds, Sue set a goal to lose weight so she could walk four blocks since she could barely walk one. Her back pain, a result of severe spinal stenosis (a narrowing of the channel around the spinal cord) left her feeling numb from the waist down any time she walked. Within five months of comprehensive weight loss, she dropped 36 pounds. "I just canceled my knee replacement because my knee feels so much better." She can now walk several blocks, no longer limited by knee pain, and has discontinued two of her four blood pressure medications. Her numbness has improved significantly.

As we've stated, the four components are essential to a comprehensive weight loss program: medical management, nutrition, activity, and education. In most discussions, you see diet and exercise as first and foremost. However, because **obesity is a medical disease,** we want to discuss the most critical element that has most often been missing: **medical management**.

You may have tried to lose weight on your own. Many, in fact, most people, can lose weight (at least a few pounds) on their own, but probably not enough to significantly improve health and to maintain weight loss.

Losing weight is a lot like paying taxes. If you do not pay any taxes, for a short time you will have more money in your pocket. However, after the IRS audit, you will end up paying back what you owed, plus penalties at an 18 percent interest rate. You are left far worse off. The same is true for unsuccessful weight loss. We will assume that you have tried to lose weight on your own, and because you are reading this, have been unsuccessful. Do not be discouraged.

Since obesity is a medical condition, it is imperative that medical management is included. In this chapter, we'll discuss the role of medical management, the qualifications, and experience of your physician, and the use of medications in making weight loss and ongoing maintenance successful.

Who should be your weight loss guide?

Some people meet with a **Registered Dietitian (RD)** who can provide you with nutritional advice. These are specialists who have received years of training and who classically have had years of experience in designing diets for critically ill hospitalized patients and others who are undernourished. However, historically most RDs get very little training in treating obesity or in the emotional difficulties that lead to diet failure.

If you do find dieticians with training in obesity treatment, they are quite effective. They can set up a meal plan and follow you during your weight loss journey. We work with some incredible dieticians who truly understand the unique issues of obesity and have been invaluable as our treatment partners. However, dieticians know that their role is only one part of the equation.

Another option for administering your program is with a **non-trained weight loss coach** or a program that uses peers or peer coaching to help you change. Weight Watchers® (WW®), for example, is led by peers who have an understanding of weight loss through their own experiences. They may have very little, if any, formal training. Weight Watchers® programs have excelled because they build a community, and establishing a community is another essential part of the weight loss journey. While some people are successful with Weight Watchers®, we've found that this approach cannot manage hunger in ways other than gently altering your nutrition or environment. People might lose 10 or 15 pounds with Weight Watchers,® but unfortunately that amount of loss is inadequate for people who have obesity.

Another option is to work with your **primary care doctor**. A primary care doctor already manages most of your medical problems and may be an expert in treating diabetes and high blood pressure, which often accompany obesity. However, most primary care physicians (except those who are obesity medicine certified) receive little to no training in the management of weight and obesity. Medical schools and residency training programs do not teach physicians how to talk to patients with obesity, how to manage both the physical and emotional consequences, or how to develop and implement an effective long-term weight loss strategy. As a result, these physicians have a difficult time managing patients with obesity. Many physicians we talk to do not even believe people can lose weight. Our data and experience show us otherwise.

Even if your doctor did receive the proper training, he or she might not have the time to coach you through your weight loss journey. Your physician is obligated to treat your high blood pressure, diabetes, high cholesterol, asthma, allergies, colds, and sinus infections. How then does he have the time needed to help you lose weight effectively? Unfortunately, most insurance companies will not reimburse your doctor to provide the type of care that works for obesity. Instead, doctors may give a quick answer: "eat less and move more." We know how that story ends: more failure, guilt, and shame.

Another expert whom you may turn to is a **certified obesity medicine physician**. After someone has received training in his or her primary field of medicine, he or she may choose to become certified in obesity medicine. The professional designation is *diplomate of the American Board of Obesity Medicine* (www.abom.org). This certification requires many hours of continuing medical education, as well as passing a board certification exam to gain recognition by the American Board of Obesity Medicine. Did you even know there were medical experts in the field of obesity?

Our experience is that certified obesity medicine physicians are best able to help you lose weight and keep it off. Certified weight loss physicians have all the most advanced and comprehensive tools at their disposal. For example, weight loss medications are a critical tool in weight management because they control hunger and the metabolic changes that occur both during weight loss and especially in maintenance. A weight loss physician has an understanding of your many and varied medical conditions and will develop a personalized plan for you.

Additionally, experts in the field of obesity medicine will not only understand your current medical conditions and those that may be contributing to weight gain, but experts will also understand health conditions for which losing weight requires close medical monitoring. For example, if you are on insulin or blood pressure medications, weight loss may lead to a rapid drop in your blood sugars or blood pressure. An obesity medicine physician has the knowledge and expertise to help you get off these medicines at the right time. If you stop these medicines too late, your blood sugars or your blood pressure may significantly decrease, causing a possible life-threatening condition.

If you discontinue them too early, you might have dangerously high blood pressure or blood sugar.

We cannot stress enough that overweight and obesity are medical diseases and not self-help problems. The fact that you cannot do it on your own is not your fault. Think of it this way: when you have knee pain, you know to see an orthopedist; when you have a heart problem, you see your cardiologist; when you have weight problems, you see your obesity medicine specialist.

As of this writing, there are almost 2,600 certified obesity medicine physicians in the United States. Fortunately, this number is increasing by 400 and 600 per year, yet is still insufficient to treat the over 100 million Americans with weight problems. Medicine has a long way to go to train enough obesity medicine specialists needed to handle all of the patients who need treatment. Fortunately, any physician can learn practical tools to manage obesity.

You can find a board certified obesity medicine physician by accessing obesitymedicine.org and clicking "Find a Clinician."

For severe obesity that does not respond adequately to medical treatment, you may consult a **bariatric surgeon** to help you lose weight. These are specialists who surgically change your anatomy to assist in weight loss. Even bariatric surgery is not a permanent cure, as many patients lose weight in the first year, only to begin to regain two to three years later. Surgery carries the risk of complications, including infection, chronic nausea and vomiting, and death. As a result, surgery should be a consideration only when nonsurgical options are ineffective. Furthermore, a comprehensive medical weight loss program will be needed to maintain the lost weight or to take over if your surgery gives incomplete weight loss.

What experience or qualifications should I look for in the professionals who treat me?

The question seems simple, but it isn't as straightforward as it may seem. Indeed, a physician has to be qualified to treat you. Additionally, you should look for a provider who has considerable real-world weight loss experience. Becoming proficient requires at least one year of experience in treating obesity full-time. More experience is better.

Also, the medical professionals and staff that are part of your team should treat you with respect. They should listen to what you have to say and take your personal opinions into account. They should not make you feel guilty or "beat you up" if you go off your plan or aren't losing as quickly as you had hoped. Many people, unfortunately, beat themselves up already, so to have a physician who shames you will cause even more harm. Though many people ask to be held to a higher standard than they hold themselves, what we have found and what the studies have shown is that a negative attitude doesn't help. Guilt and shame lead to overeating in an attempt to self-medicate those feelings. Then patients end up feeling even worse because they made poor choices and overeat even more. The cycle can be endless. Keeping an upbeat attitude, staying positive, and looking for better solutions the next time is more effective-and feels a lot better!

Betsy had been away from the clinic for several months. We wanted to put her on medicine and asked her if it would be OK for us to call her physician to discuss initiating medicine for weight loss. We also wanted to ask her family physician if it would interact with her other medication. She quickly said, "The reason I don't talk about this with my primary physician is he is that person who said, 'Just eat less and move more.'" Many physicians tell patients not to take weight loss medications because they may be "dangerous." While every medicine, including acetaminophen (Tylenol®), has potential side effects, it is rare that the side effects of weight loss medications are more dangerous than having obesity, a disease which contributes to innumerable heart attacks, cancer, need for joint replacements from arthritis, lung disease, and other dangerous conditions.

We look forward to a time when the medical community treats obesity seriously. We would all agree our health deserves it!

Is it essential to see a certified obesity medicine specialist?

Sara has been overweight since the age of 18 when she started college. She had been active as a tennis player in high school but stopped when she attended college. After gaining 18 pounds her first year of college, she went to Weight Watchers®. She lost five pounds that summer but put on six more pounds in her second year of college. After college, she went to a naturopathic doctor (NMD) who prescribed HCG injections and a 500–calorie diet consisting of two chicken breasts, one serving of fruit, a serving of vegetables, and one slice of bread. She lost eight pounds her first week. But each week she stayed on the plan, she felt weaker and weaker. So her naturopath advised her to stop exercising. After four weeks, she had lost 20 pounds and went out to dinner with her family. She ate three slices of bread, a steak, and salad, and her fatigue immediately improved. The following day, she could not push herself to get back

Chasing Diets

on the diet. Less than three months later, she regained all of the 20 pounds lost plus an additional five pounds. Sara's story is a common one.

An NMD is not a medical doctor in the way you might think. They usually prescribe herbal homeopathic substances not approved by the FDA. Most of these products have not undergone the rigorous studies needed for the FDA to allow them to be dispensed by a pharmacy with a physician's prescription.

Every herbal and homeopathic product must carry this label: "This statement has not been evaluated by the Food and Drug Administration. This product is not intended to diagnose, treat, cure, or prevent any disease." How can a product be allowed to make claims while putting that label on it? We recommend you be highly skeptical. **Check out the ingredients on a reputable site such as www.examine.com.**

A nonprofessional who uses herbal and homeopathic medications does not have the experience in treating obesity and its complications. He may not be able to manage your blood pressure and tell you when to stop medications when weight loss reduces your hypertension. He or she may not be able to tell you when and how much to cut your insulin since weight loss can drop your blood sugars quite quickly.

Overtreatment of diabetes can be dangerous, leading to weakness, confusion, and loss of consciousness.

Our advice is to find a treatment that works, delivered by a provider who is trained in weight management; to lose weight quickly; and then to stay on a life-long maintenance plan. Finding a method that controls your hunger and allows you a lifestyle that is working for you (with or without medication) is the most effective approach to treating your weight condition.

The more medical concerns or diseases you have, or more times you have tried to diet in the past, the more critical it is to seek a professional who has dedicated his or her career to treating overweight.

How should physicians speak with me about my weight issues?

One of the most essential tools a weight loss physician has is his communication style. Traditionally, doctors are taught to provide "informed consent." Informed consent means that your doctor tells you that if you do or do not do something, something good or bad will happen. For example, if your doctor says to you, "If you don't lose weight, you'll develop heart disease, stroke, arthritis, and ultimately, you may die." You might become fearful and defensive, and tell him or her all the reasons you can't lose weight. You might even list for your doctor all the various diet plans you have tried and how likely you are to fail in a new endeavor. You will likely end up leaving the office feeling quite discouraged. Your doctor will probably regret ever bringing up the conversation, having left you feeling hopeless and unlikely to return. For this reason, many physicians avoid the discussion of weight altogether.

Imagine, on the other hand, if your doctor understands the struggles that you have had losing weight and gives you hope that there is treatment for your condition. Your doctor will ask you what your goals are, and with you, create a treatment plan that you can follow. Your doctor will agree to change that plan as your life or health changes. Finally, your doctor will give you hope that you can keep your weight off because that physician has an understanding that weight conditions are a chronic disease. Any new change in your life, such as a new job, injury, and even big vacation, tends to cause challenges to your weight loss plan. An expert physician will help you manage those times. Most important, your weight loss physician will be there to help you keep the weight off, which is ultimately the goal. By losing weight, by improving your health, and having a plan that works for you, you can see long-term success.

Even if a primary care physician does not have the expertise, he can work with your obesity medicine specialist to be an excellent guide on the weight loss journey. We advise healthcare providers to ask patients, "Do you want help with your weight?" and to then stop and listen. If the patient wants help, the primary care physician can refer the patient to a respected obesity medicine specialist. The point is that the power to choose rests in the hands of the patient.

Are medications a part of a weight loss program, and if so, are they safe?

The answer is simple. Yes, medications are part of many successful weight loss programs, and this is one of the most important reasons to work with a physician. It is indeed up to you and your physician to decide whether specialized treatment is right for you.

When you consider obesity as a disease, medications are a tool, as in the case of high blood pressure or high cholesterol.

As previously discussed, weight loss leads to changes in the hormones leptin and ghrelin that ensure an increase in hunger. They are continually trying to drive us back to our initial higher weight. Our bodies act as if there is a famine in the world around us. Our bodies cannot tell the difference between diet and starvation.

Hunger has a voice. Imagine a tiny person sitting on your shoulder with a megaphone who can talk or yell in your ear. When you are at your initial (high) weight, the person isn't saying anything. As you start to lose a few pounds, the tiny person starts speaking very softly, "Please eat! Please eat!" Then as you lose ten or fifteen pounds, it starts getting louder and louder, "Eat, eat." When you get to 25 and 50 pounds, it gets even louder, "EAT! EAT!" Weight loss medicines do not stop the signals, but rather, mask them. Weight loss medicines figuratively cover your ears from that tiny person yelling in your ear. Even though that tiny person is still telling you to eat, it is a lot easier for your brain to ignore the voice.

How long should I stay on weight loss medications?

If drug therapy is helping you, there is no reason why you should stop weight loss medication. Like a blood pressure medicine, if your blood pressure is in control through medication, and tomorrow you stop taking it, the following day your blood pressure may elevate to dangerous levels. The same thing happens with our appetite and our weight. If we're taking a medication that is helping us adhere to our plan and all of the sudden we stop the medication, appetite will increase, and our weight will go up.

You and your doctor decide if lifelong weight loss medication treatment is needed. Each patient is different.

Sometimes we recommend that you remain on your medication for at least six to twelve months. At the end of this period, if you want to stop the medicine, your doctor may stop or taper the medication, depending on which drug you are taking. If you can stay within five pounds of your goal weight, you will likely be able to remain off that medication. A high level of exercise, close follow-up with your clinic, and frequent small meals will give you the best chances of maintaining weight loss. If you stay within that five-pound zone while off the medication, you are doing well and do not need to continue the medication.

For any weight gain over five pounds, alarms should go off, and we advise you to resume that weight loss medication. Experience shows us that weight gain of five pounds often leads to more rapid weight gain.

What are my medication options?

Because medications are an invaluable component of many successful weight loss programs, physicians will choose a drug dependent upon several factors: age, previous weight loss attempts, type of hunger (body hunger versus cravings), the presence of heart disease, diabetes or high blood pressure, previous bariatric surgery, and history of depression. In some instances, more than one medication may be combined to provide optimal effect with the least side effects.

Adipex®/Phentermine. Phentermine is the most commonly prescribed weight loss medication. Phentermine is a mild stimulant and acts to reduce appetite by acting on the hypothalamus, as well as increasing metabolism by five to 10%. Phentermine received approval in 1959 for a limited period of 12 weeks. At that time, obesity was considered an acute illness, much like strep throat or a sinus infection. If you have such an infection, you take antibiotic medication for a limited time, usually ten days. You do not need to continue the medication because the treatment results in a cure. Unfortunately, obesity doesn't work this way.

In the 1990s, doctors combined phentermine with fenfluramine, a combination that was called "phen-fen." Fenfluramine is a strong and non-selective serotonin agonist, which means it stimulates serotonin receptors. There are serotonin receptors in the brain, but also on the heart valves, and these high doses of fenfluramine led to growths on the heart, leading to leaky heart valves. Fear of dangerous side effects spilled over to the use of all weight loss medications. It also resulted in several class action lawsuits. The FDA banned Fenfluramine; however, phentermine (the other half of phen/fen) withstood the scrutiny and was then (and is now) agreed to be a very safe medication.

The use of phentermine long-term has been a controversial subject. Weight loss physicians have become quite comfortable with long-term use, although its use for more than 12 weeks is not approved by the FDA and as a result, is considered "off-label" use. As phentermine is now an inexpensive, generic medication, it will likely never be FDA-approved for long-term use because of the expense of studies to change the FDA label. Studies by Ed Hendricks and others show that long-term use of phentermine rarely, if ever, leads to dependency. As a result, it is generally felt to be safe. Again, its use for more than a 12-week period is off-label and therefore, should only be prescribed by experienced physicians.

Common side effects of phentermine include dry mouth and insomnia. More severe side effects such as increased heart rate, anxiety, or increased blood pressure are less likely. Dry mouth can promote increased fluid intake, which is important during weight loss anyway. Patients with coronary artery disease or severe arrhythmias should avoid phentermine.

Qsymia®/Phentermine plus Topiramate (ER) extended release. Qsymia® is a brand name medication that contains two medicines that have been available for decades, phentermine and topiramate—in a long-acting formulation. Interestingly, while phentermine is not approved for long-term use, Qsymia® (which contains phentermine) is FDA-approved for long-term use. The combination of these two medications together leads to more significant weight loss than either one of the components by itself, an action called synergy. Phentermine works by lowering appetite and raising metabolism while topiramate acts to reduce hunger through one neurotransmitter pathway, the GABA system. Topiramate also has a calming effect and may also help with sleep. Topiramate is useful in patients who experience weight regain after bariatric surgery.

Qsymia® has multiple fixed-dose combinations. Most of the time, your physician will start you on the lowest dose for a week or two and gradually increase. Common side effects to Qsymia® relate to each component. In addition to the side effects mentioned above with phentermine, topiramate can cause sedation and, less likely, memory change (primarily, difficulty in word finding) or depression. Topamax can increase the risk of kidney stones, so you should advise your physician if you have a previous history of kidney stone disease. Also, tell your doctor if you have glaucoma.

Tenuate®/Diethylpropion. Tenuate® is a milder and shorter-acting stimulant than phentermine. It both lowers appetite and raises metabolism. It can be used by itself or in combination with phentermine. It is especially helpful for evening hunger since it lasts just a few hours. The most common side effects of diethylpropion include insomnia (less often), anxiety, and elevated blood pressure or heart rate, which need to be monitored. Like phentermine, there are certain people who should not use diethylpropion, including people with significant coronary artery disease and chronic heart arrhythmia.

Bontril®/Phendimetrazine. Phendimetrazine works both by raising metabolism and reducing appetite. It is a stimulant and comes in a short and long-acting version. Since it is a stimulant, it should be avoided in patients with heart arrhythmias or heart disease. Side effects include anxiety, insomnia, increased blood pressure, and elevated heart rate. Because it is a DEA schedule three medication (slightly higher potential for dependency), it is more highly controlled by the FDA. For this reason, patients need to be monitored closely for side effects.

Contrave® /Bupropion plus Naltrexone extended release. Contrave® is a combination of bupropion and naltrexone. This drug is a non-stimulant medication that is particularly helpful for appetite and cravings. Bupropion (generic for Wellbutrin®) is an antidepressant. Therefore, those with low mood and low energy often see improvement in these conditions. The other component, naltrexone, acts to enhance the effect of bupropion. Certain people should not use this medication, in particular, those who have severe anxiety and those who have seizure disorders. Patients taking opiate-class pain-relieving medications should not take Contrave® since naltrexone blocks the effects of opiates and could cause medication withdrawal. Contrave® is FDA-approved for long-term use. Since it is not a stimulant, it can be used safely in patients with heart disease.

Wellbutrin® (bupropion) is also prescribed for smoking cessation and naltrexone for alcohol cessation. When taken together, the combination helps with food cravings. The most common side effect of Contrave® is nausea, which occurs in one out of every three people. In trials of Contrave®, only three to four percent of patients had to stop the medicine because of nausea.

Belviq®/Lorcaserin. Belviq® works directly on the appetite centers in the brain. Its molecule is similar to serotonin, one of the common brain neurotransmitters. Stimulation of the brain serotonin receptor reduces appetite. Belviq acts on those serotonin receptors. Since it does not affect metabolism, it is also safe to use in patients with heart disease. Studies show that half of the patients who take Belviq® experience decreased appetite and weight loss, and the other half gain no significant benefit.

Belviq® is similar to fenfluramine (the one that damages heart valves). But, the Belviq® molecule is very specific for the brain serotonin receptor without acting on the heart serotonin receptor. Therefore, it should not affect the heart valves. In the studies of Belviq®, over 30,000 echocardiograms were done showing that it did not damage heart valves. Further data from a cardiovascular outcomes trial confirmed the safety of Belviq®.

While Belviq® by itself is a modest appetite suppressor, it has enhanced effect when added to weight loss medications that have different mechanisms. Studies showed no increase in heart attacks or strokes in overweight and obese patients at high risk of such events.

Saxenda®/Liraglutide. Saxenda® (Liraglutide) is similar to a chemical made in our bodies, glucagon-like peptide one (GLP-1). GLP-1 results in both lower appetite and decreased blood sugars. Natural GLP-1 is secreted from the small intestine, travels through the blood, and is taken up by the brain, specifically the hypothalamus. In its naturally occurring state, the GLP-1 effect lasts 60-120 seconds before being broken down. The body has to keep sending more up to the brain to signal feelings of fullness. This modified synthetic version lasts much longer, with a half-life of 13 hours, allowing for once-a-day fine needle injection.

The side effects of Saxenda® include nausea, diarrhea, and occasional headaches. It should not be used in people who have certain types of thyroid cancers or family history of multiple endocrine neoplasia, a rare genetic cancer. It should also not be used in patients with a history of pancreatitis as it may slightly increase the risk of pancreatitis

GLP-1 analogs have great promise in the management of obesity and diabetes. Future versions of GLP-1 drugs will be more potent and require less frequent administration.

Xenical®/Orlistat. Xenical® acts to reduce fat absorption in the intestine. This medication blocks the gut enzyme lipoprotein lipase, which is required to break down fat into smaller components needed for digestion. This drug causes the body to absorb 30% less of the fat one eats. Overeating fat leads to increased gas, greasy diarrhea (steatorrhea), and bloating. In our experience, Xenical® has limited use in the treatment of obesity due to limited weight loss and the diarrhea side effect.

When we first started practicing weight loss in the early 2000s, there were only two drugs commonly being used for weight loss. Xenical® was one of them. Early in our experience with this drug, Jenny, a 58-year-old female office-worker had an unpleasant side effect. One day while at her desk, she thought she was passing gas only to discover that she passed loose stool. She had to go home in the middle of the day and change clothes. She never retook Xenical®!

Off-Label Medications. Certain non-weight loss drugs aid in weight loss. These medicines are considered "off-label." Many drugs are useful in the treatment of diseases but are not FDA-approved. In such cases, it is common for the physicians to use best-practices, the experience of the community that treats that condition, and small pilot studies to determine what is best for a patient.

For example, studies on **metformin** (Glucophage®) have shown it to be useful for weight loss, but it is FDA-approved for diabetes. Metformin is a medication that reduces appetite by raising the body's natural levels of GLP-1, reducing the absorption of sugar, and decreasing the liver's production of sugar. By having slower production and less sugar absorption, the body makes less insulin. This action leads to increases in insulin sensitivity and leads to a lower tendency to build body fat. Metformin also appears to have anti-carcinogenic (anti-cancer) properties.

In a large trial, the Diabetes Prevention Program (DPP) Study, metformin was shown to be highly effective in preventing prediabetes from progressing to diabetes, the leading cause of acquired blindness and kidney failure.

Additionally, metformin was shown in studies of teenagers to be helpful in weight loss. In these studies, the teens did not have elevated sugar or diabetes, and the metformin was used only for weight loss.

Metformin is inexpensive and well-tolerated. A minority of persons taking metformin experience nausea or diarrhea. The extended-release (XL) form has fewer side effects. Rarely, metformin can lead to an electrolyte disturbance called metabolic acidosis. Metabolic acidosis is quite serious and is most likely to occur in people with already significantly impaired kidney function or in patients who are severely dehydrated. Therefore, it is essential to drink adequate fluid while on this medication.

How much fluid should you drink while on metformin? We generally recommend drinking enough fluids to keep your urine clear. If your urine is medium to dark yellow, we strongly advise increasing your fluid intake.

Topiramate is useful with or without phentermine. As mentioned above, the combination of topiramate with phentermine comprises the weight loss drug Qsymia®. Alone, topiramate has no stimulatory effect, so it is quite useful in people who have an anxiety disorder, suffer from insomnia, or those who have other reasons to take topiramate such as migraine headaches.

A significant advantage of undergoing treatment by a physician with expertise in obesity is that successful weight loss and maintenance often requires weight loss medications. Full knowledge of your medical history, medications, drug sensitivities, and allergies is critical when considering which medicine to use and for how long. Weight loss drugs counteract the adverse changes in leptin and ghrelin that increase hunger and lower metabolism. Without these medications as part of a treatment plan, successful weight loss is virtually impossible for some people.

What are the surgical procedures used for weight loss?

The least invasive weight loss procedures are the **laparoscopic band** (lap band) and the endoscopically placed balloon, which change the amount of food allowed in the stomach. We now understand that hunger is more strongly linked to hormonal factors than to stomach size. Because the restriction from the lap band does nothing to control appetite and does not result in consistent weight loss, this surgery has lost popularity. Complication rates of this procedure exceed the benefits. Some 50% or more of patients eventually need to remove the band due to reflux esophagitis (heartburn), erosions (the band can cut into and become surrounded by the stomach lining), difficulty eating foods such as chicken breast, band slippage, or lack of weight loss.

A more aggressive procedure is the **gastric sleeve**. This surgery removes part of your stomach, which, in turn, reduces the levels of ghrelin. One downside with this surgery is that those who have heartburn (gastroesophageal reflux disease or GERD) will likely experience worse symptoms after the procedure.

Although this procedure has become the most commonly performed bariatric procedure in the US, the durability of its effect is under scrutiny. Months after the surgery, some patients begin to regain weight as hunger increases, possibly due to increases in ghrelin.

When it comes to weight gain, our bodies will always seek a way to regain weight! We have a fantastic ability to survive. Starvation in first world countries is rare, and there are many safeguards built into our bodies to prevent this.

Before the popularity of gastric sleeve, **gastric bypass surgery** (formally called a **Roux-en-Y gastric bypass**) was the most common surgical procedure. It is one the most effective bariatric surgical procedures. Bypass surgery both reduces the size of the stomach and changes the anatomy of the intestines to cause malabsorption. We now know that bypass surgery causes the gut to secrete hormones that send signals to the brain to reduce appetite. These signals affect the brain just like weight loss medications.

Bypass surgery leads to marked and longer-lasting weight loss than the previously discussed procedures, yet some people begin to regain weight several years later. It is for this reason that long-term follow-up and a medical plan is required. Side effects of gastric bypass include infection, bowel obstruction, leakage, and death (rarely) in the short term. Long-term effects include nausea, vomiting, and diarrhea. If you are considering a bariatric surgical procedure, this is the procedure, in our opinion, with the best benefit-to-risk ratio.

The most aggressive procedure is the **duodenal switch**, cutting out most of the stomach and rearranging the small intestine. This surgery is used in patients with very high BMI's (above 50), and has a rate of death of 2%. This procedure leads to marked weight loss and malabsorption. Because of the complications, this procedure is done only when all other options have been exhausted.

Chapter 4: The Second Leg: Nutrition

DANNY: "MY NUTRITION for a typical day would begin with a heavy carb-based breakfast, usually a bagel or toast and coffee. I snacked during the work day, and lunch and dinner tended to be large portions of food—lasagna, tacos, spaghetti. Typically, I'd have a burger with a couple of slices of cheese plus bacon and mayo, with fries or tater tots. As for vegetables, I opted for corn with butter. At night I generally found myself back in the kitchen to grab a few cookies or a bowl of ice cream. Or I'd add a piece of fruit because that was 'healthy.' Also, I could always justify what I ate by having a salad—but that salad was

loaded with bacon bits, cheese, and ranch dressing. I learned a lot about nutrition through the program, and learned that it is a major component of a long-term weight loss plan."

The second component of a comprehensive weight loss program, after medical management, is nutrition. Any successful diet must contain all of the essential macro and micronutrients required for the body to function.

We will discuss each of these essential elements here and why each is essential to health.

Protein. Protein is essential to nearly every body function, including healing, making hormones, building muscle and bone, replacing cells that break down, making blood cells, and growing hair and nails. If people do not get sufficient protein in their diets, the body will consume muscle using the amino acids for these functions. Proteins from milk and animal meat contain the highest amounts of **essential amino acids**, called such because the body cannot produce these acids on its own. Plant-based proteins (soy, pea, rice, and wheat proteins, for example) contain fewer essential amino acids, and therefore, people need to eat more of them to get the same amount of essential amino acids.

Essential fatty acids. These are important for the production of sex hormones (estrogen, progesterone, and testosterone), stress hormones (cortisol), and skin growth. Deficiencies will cause rashes, poor sexual function, and loss of menses. There are two long chain fatty acids, linoleic and alpha-linolenic acid, and these can only be obtained from foods we eat.

Vitamins and minerals. Too numerous to mention individually, vitamins are required for everything, including normal vision (vitamin A), heart and brain function (B vitamins), skin and hair health (vitamin C), and bone strength (vitamin D). Minerals are also required for many body functions, such as red blood cell production (iron).

Trace elements. Trace elements are catalysts that make enzymes work properly. These include copper, iodine, selenium, and chromium. Tiny amounts suffice here.

Electrolytes. Electrolytes are critical to maintaining blood pressure and fluid balance (sodium), heart and muscle function (potassium), and bone function (calcium). Our body closely monitors these levels, and an imbalance in some of these can cause the heart to stop, the brain to swell, and even death.

Water. Water is one of the essential components of our diet, and even a small deficit in body fluids can lead to shock, kidney failure, and death.

Fiber. Fiber is needed to keep normal bowel mobility, and lack of fiber will lead to constipation or diarrhea.

For a diet to be healthy, it must provide all of the above essential nutrients. Note that carbohydrates and other sugars are not necessary. Our bodies can make all of the sugar we need as long as our food contains enough protein.

Is "one-size-fits-all" is a myth?

For you to answer the question of what is the best nutrition plan for you, we must first submit that **no single diet fits everyone.** The best diet is the one that you successfully use to help you lose weight, keep it off, and improve health.

Our inherited DNA determines many aspects of weight control. There are at least 200 genes that control our weight, usually by affecting appetite or metabolism. Since we receive one set of genes from each parent, we have two slightly different copies. If one of those genes causes weight gain, it often overrules the normal one.

Keeping this in mind, having a single overweight parent doubles the risk of developing obesity. If both parents have obesity, their children have at least a 90% chance of having obesity. We have many genes that cause severe weight gain but few that lead to significant weight loss. Perhaps the survival of our species depended upon it at one time.

When people say, "I think I'm overweight because … (fill in the blank)," the reasons are often varied. Sometimes they eat too many carbohydrates; sometimes they do not eat enough protein, eat too late in the day, skip breakfast, avoid exercise, or get inadequate sleep. All those answers are correct and relate directly to genetic make-up. These genes indeed regulate fat loss, metabolism, hunger and all the other systems involved with weight control.

Which plan should I choose?

There are many diets to choose from, and we'll spend some time outlining each one.

Low Fat Diet. These diets include Dash, Ornish, and Zone diets. These low-fat diets became popular during the 1970s and 80s as a result of skyrocketing rates of heart disease. Government health officials felt pressured to do something to control this epidemic. Physicians discovered that fatty cholesterol deposits in major arteries caused heart attacks. Furthermore, blood cholesterol levels correlated with these plaques. They assumed that the ingestion of cholesterol and fat was the cause of these clogged arteries. The conclusion at the time was that a high-fat diet caused high cholesterol.

While there was no definitive science behind this approach, the low-fat diet was born. The theory was, "Eat less fat, and we'll have less fatty plaques in our arteries." This belief was false, yet the recommendation to eat less fat and cholesterol persisted for many years. This belief led to an explosion of diets filled with grains and other high-carbohydrate foods.

Some people lose weight on low-fat diets; however, those responders are the minority. The reason it doesn't work for most is that when you restrict fat, you tend to eat more carbohydrates. Eliminating a food group often causes us to make up the difference elsewhere. As a result, when you eat those carbs, you drive your pancreas to release insulin, and insulin drives sugar into your fat cells where you store the sugar as fat.

Studies after one year show a total weight loss of three pounds on the Ornish diet and seven pounds on the Zone diet. Due to this small amount of weight loss, we recommend a low-fat approach for only a minority of people with obesity.

Very Low Carbohydrate Diets. These are diets such as Atkins, South Beach, ketogenic (or keto for short), protein sparing modified fast, and Dukan diets. These diets markedly restrict sugars and other carbohydrates, since the latter are converted to simple sugars when absorbed during digestion. The South Beach Diet® essentially starts with a very low or low carbohydrate diet; however, it contains fewer processed foods. There are usually three phases of the South Beach Diet. The first one lasts one to two weeks with a very low carbohydrate-based diet. In phase two, carbohydrates increase. In phase three carbohydrates increase further, and portion control dominates. People lose weight in phases one and two, and unfortunately gradually gain weight back in phase three. Well-controlled studies are lacking on long-term weight loss with the South Beach Diet.

Very low carbohydrate diets work partially by suppressing insulin levels resulting in the breakdown of fat. Since sugar is not readily available, fat becomes the preferred fuel. Ketogenic diets contain less than 50 grams of carbohydrate per day. As long as we supply adequate amounts of protein, sugar is a nonessential nutrient. Low carbohydrate diets (from the breakdown of fat) lead the body to generate ketones, which by themselves suppress appetite. Studies show approximately 10.4-pound long-term weight loss when utilized alone. As with many self-help diets, the results are limited.

However, these paltry results change when combined with other tools, such as more intensive behavioral therapy, close physician guidance, and weight loss medications. Low carbohydrate diets have become the mainstay of many medical weight loss programs for a good reason. Carbohydrates cause inflammation such as swelling of the lining of blood vessels, making the blood vessels sticky, resulting in plaque buildup. Due to the beneficial effects on appetite, blood sugar, cholesterol, and other risk factors for heart disease, very low carbohydrate diets are the diet of choice by many obesity medicine specialists. A strong thumbs-up.

Intermittent fasting. In intermittent fasting, you restrict or eliminate food intake for a period. There are many different variants of intermittent fasting diets. In one version you do not eat anything for 36 hours, followed by a free, unrestricted meal. In another version, time-restricted feeding, you eat only once per day in a three, six, or eight-hour period. The data is somewhat controversial on whether intermittent fasting is a successful weight loss method.

Philosophically, we struggle with the concept of intermittent fasting, because our bodies have an ongoing need for nutrition, especially protein. When you eliminate protein, and your body has continuous needs for protein, your body will cannibalize muscle to undergo the necessary functions of living. Thus, we would expect intermittent fasting would lead to a loss of lean body mass and muscle. The last thing you would want to lose is muscle mass since building muscle is difficult, and a loss of muscle mass will lead to a slower resting metabolism. Some physicians believe that fasting preserves muscle better than calorie-restricted diets, and we look forward to more studies regarding fasting. It would be beneficial and preferential to live off fat and protect muscle during times of famine, but unfortunately, there is not, as yet, sufficient data to support this theory.

HCG Diet. The Human Chorionic Gonadotropin (HCG) diet was first described in the 1950s by an endocrinologist, Albert Simeons. Dr. Simeons treated boys who had a pituitary tumor preventing them from entering into puberty. When used in an injectable form, HCG raises testosterone and estrogen. When receiving HCG, these boy's testosterone levels elevated as they went into puberty. As a result, the boys grew, matured, and lost weight. This led Dr. Simeons to erroneously hypothesize that HCG in combination with a 500 calorie diet successfully treats obesity.

The 500-calorie diet is quite strict, usually consisting of two chicken breasts per day, a salad or two, a small apple and a rusk—which is hard, cracker-like bread. Most anyone can lose weight on a 500-calorie diet; the problem with this method is that you do not know what you are losing. Are you losing just fat? Are you losing muscle? Although individuals lose weight quickly on this diet, in our experience most of these dieters regain more weight than they lose.

Those who supervise HCG diets advised patients not to exercise, which is probably a good thing if you are only on a 500 calorie diet. Not exercising is opposite of what the substantial majority of physicians believe to be healthy. We all lose some muscle as we lose weight, but lack of exercise enhances loss of muscle mass. Other risks to HCG diets result from increased estrogen levels. The elevated estrogen increases the risk of blood clots in the legs and pulmonary embolisms (blood clots in the lungs), and increases the risk of breast cancer.

In the 1950s, little was known about the science of ketosis or the philosophy that ketogenic diets can suppress appetite. Some believed that it was the HCG shot that was helping people control hunger. Multiple controlled and double-blinded studies have not shown that HCG has contributed to weight loss or hunger control. In reality, it is the diet that causes the weight loss and HCG is just a placebo, like taking a sugar pill, or in this case a sugar shot!

Some people who use the HCG diet recommend oral HCG instead of injection, which is even more preposterous. HCG in its oral form is broken down in the stomach and never actually reaches the bloodstream. Therefore, it absolutely cannot aid in either weight loss or hunger control.

Initially, people on HCG diets may feel better because of the low carbohydrate intake. The ketones that are released provide a feeling of euphoria, or well-being, in some. A significant concern is that the HCG diet is not at all sustainable. A 500 calorie diet by its very nature does not teach someone the skills of lifelong weight management.

As a result of the lack of studies showing that HCG assists at all in weight loss, three influential organizations, the American Medical Association (AMA); the Obesity Medicine Association; and The Obesity Society each have published position statements against HCG. They advise against HCG as a tool for weight loss and also against the Simeons' (500 calorie) diet.

The FDA has also recommended HCG not be used for weight loss and has threatened closing clinics that use HCG. Any diet that is lacking nutrients will lead to malnutrition. The HCG diet certainly qualifies as a diet that does not provide all the nutrients required. In our experience, the longer someone is on an HCG diet, the paler they look and the weaker they feel. It is just not healthy or safe.

In summary, we give HCG thumbs down.

Paleo Diet. Paleo is a diet that has become popular because it is believed to be natural. The concept is that we should eat like cavemen, eating only foods that are unprocessed and were available to hunters and gatherers. Paleo diet is high in meat, vegetables, nuts, and fruit. They are devoid of processed foods. A Paleo diet does not usually rely on calorie restriction and can, therefore, be either low or high calorie, so it may not lead to weight loss.

There indeed is limited evidence that this what the caveman or hunter/gatherer society ate. In that time, people only lived to the age of 30, versus 80 and 90 years that we tend to now, so it cannot be considered a longevity diet.

The Paleo diet is very labor intensive. Paleo dieters often spend several hours on weekends food prepping for the week. Because the diet requires all fresh fruits, vegetables, and meats, it can be very expensive. Rigorous studies on long-term weight loss on Paleo diets are lacking, so it is too early to recommend this diet approach.

Mediterranean Diet. The Mediterranean diet promotes foods that are available in Italy and Greece. It consists of less processed foods, emphasis on fish, nuts, fruits and vegetables, and little red meat. Through Blue Zone research, studies of people whose populations have large numbers of people who live over 100, Mediterranean diets appear to improve longevity. Mediterranean diets have benefits, including lower risk factors for heart disease such as lower LDL "bad" cholesterol and lower risks for cancer. Mediterranean diets again can be higher or lower in calories and do not reliably lead to weight loss. Studies on Mediterranean diets show an average of 9.7-pound weight loss.

Because of the improvements in health risk factors, we give a thumbs-up rating to Mediterranean diets. Furthermore, weight loss of these diets when combined with comprehensive medical management is likely to be greater.

Weight Watchers®. Weight Watchers®, now called WW®, uses a point system as a means of nutritionally budgeting intake over the day. Dieters are allowed a limited number of points tracked either with paper, website, or smartphone application. Foods with high calories, especially those high in fat have the most points; whereas, certain very low or non-fat foods are considered "free" and allowed in unlimited amounts. Those foods include many vegetables, eggs, chicken breast, beans, peas, and other legumes, fruit, and yogurt. This list notably contains higher calorie foods, such as artichoke hearts and higher sugar fruits and vegetables including mangoes, melons, and corn. Grapes are also free, and we have seen patients eat one pound of grapes per day because they are "healthy." The original version of Weight Watchers® included peer support groups, which added a level of accountability lacking in the online version. Controlled studies show a weight loss of 6.6 pounds at one year, but the newer versions with an excess of free foods and lack of support will likely decrease the amount of weight loss.

The Gluten-free diet. Gluten is the protein contained in wheat. It is what causes flour to be sticky, important in bread and baked goods. Gluten has been blamed for everything from depression, fatigue, headache and brain fog to obesity (In fact, true gluten intolerance probably leads to weight loss!). Reducing gluten intake will result in weight loss as long as you limit other carbohydrates and overall calories. The reduction of carbs in any form will undoubtedly assist with weight loss; however, we do not have sufficient evidence showing that eliminating gluten alone will lead to weight loss.

One percent of our society has gluten intolerance, a condition called **celiac disease**. Celiac disease is a severe allergy to the protein present in wheat gluten. Eating gluten causes those with celiac disease to develop an intense reaction. The lining of the intestine sloughs off, leading to severe diarrhea, abdominal bloating, and blood in the stools. Celiac disease is a dangerous medical condition requiring the care of a gastroenterologist. The evaluation includes a thorough history, physical examination, intestinal endoscopy with biopsies, and also blood tests to measure the antibodies specific to the disease. The vast majority of people who think they're gluten intolerant do not have celiac disease.

Gluten intolerance affects only 1% of the population, indicated by bloody diarrhea and weight loss when eating wheat-containing foods. Reducing gluten only helps with weight loss if you also reduce other carbohydrates.

From the standpoint of weight loss, removing gluten in the absence of celiac disease is ineffective. The problem with gluten-free diets is that people who avoid gluten end up replacing wheat-based carbohydrates with non-wheat carbohydrates. For example, when preparing gluten-free baked goods such as bread, cookies, and pastries, chefs add rice flour instead of regular (wheat) flour. Rice flour has a higher glycemic index—it results in a faster blood sugar rise than regular flour does. A healthier approach would be to reduce all carbohydrates—those that contain wheat flour, rice flour, and other starches, as well as simple sugars. Weight loss studies on gluten-free diets are lacking. In summary, we do not favor gluten-free regimens for weight loss.

Meal Replacements. Meal replacements are foods that are designed to contain a high amount of nutrition and a low amount of calories. They usually come in the form of shakes, soups, or bars, and require little or no preparation. The advantages of meal replacements are the following:

- **Pre-portioned and calorie controlled.** They come in single serving size, so the user gets exactly the intended amount of calories, no more and no less. Single meal packets make it harder to overeat. No matter how good we think we are at measuring foods while we're at home or in restaurants (where portions are markedly size-distorted), it is tough to eat precisely the calories that you are trying to eat.

For example, consider that a chicken breast is very healthy when you are eating a standard serving size. If you eat four chicken breasts in a meal, that surely wouldn't be as healthy. With meal replacements, we know the portion is typically one package whether that be a bar, shake, or soup.

- **Stimuli-narrowing.** By having a limited number of choices, the dieter will have less temptation to overeat. For example, when you go to a restaurant, you order a single entree. When you go to a buffet, you will be more likely to eat three or more entrees, plus appetizers and desserts. You may eat so much that you will leave feeling overly stuffed and ill.

  When given a limited amount of flavors, you narrow the different types of stimuli that your brain is getting for food. Think about it. When choosing a favorite restaurant with fifty choices on the menu, you could eat a different item every single day—and you probably would. You will likely eat larger portions as well.

- **High nutritional value.** It is easier to get all of the nutrients, especially protein, without getting excess carbohydrates and fat that pack on the calories. Plus, with meal replacements, one serving can provide all of the vitamins and minerals you need.

- **Very filling.** Meal replacements contain all that you need, so they make you feel more full. Our body is quite adept at ensuring we crave the nutrients we lack, sometimes to our detriment. When children lack iron in their diets, they develop anemia, the inability to make enough red blood cells. Iron-deficient children will crave iron-containing foods and develop pica—the eating of dirt.

Meal replacement diets come in two forms: **non-medical**, those you can purchase over-the-counter from standard grocery stores and through multilevel marketing companies, and **medical**, which require a prescription from a health care provider.

- **Non-medical meal replacements** include Slim Fast®, Atkins shakes®, and Premier Protein® and are a helpful tool for weight maintenance because they are more filling and contain fewer calories. They also provide needed structure to a nutritional plan. These are calorie-controlled and contain most but not all of the nutrients required for health.

> *Non-medical meal replacements can be purchased without a medical prescription and do not contain all essential nutrients. As a result, they should not be used as the sole source of food.*

Because they lack some nutrients, non-medical meal replacements must be combined with whole food. As a result, the total calorie intake will be higher, usually 1200 calories or more. You cannot live for more than a short while on solely over-the-counter meal replacements; you have to vary your diet for additional nutrients and will ultimately have to increase your calorie intake.

Studies have shown that the use of meal replacements in weight maintenance is quite effective. The Look AHEAD study is a decade-long analysis of the use of meal replacements. This remarkable trial studied over 5000 patients with diabetes, half who used meal replacement shakes and half who had usual diabetes care (the control group). A total of 96% of patients completed the study, and average weight loss was 8.6% of total body weight in the patients using meal replacements, compared to only 0.7% in the control group. Further, the more meal replacements people used in maintenance (three per day versus one or fewer per day), the more weight they kept off over the ten years of the study.

- **Medical meal replacements** are very different from over-the-counter meal replacements. These are made by medical companies (OPTIFAST® from Nestle Health Sciences, HealthOne® from Health Nutrition Technology, New Directions® from Robard®, Bariatrix®, Bariatric Advantage®, and HMR®). Medical meal replacements are usually purchased directly from the physician administering the diet. Calorie intake with these products is as low as 600 to 800 calories per day, so weight loss is fast. Studies on the use of medical meal replacements show an average of 46.6 pounds weight loss at six months and 40 pounds at one year.

  Medical meal replacements are different in that they not only have all essential macronutrients such as protein and essential fatty acids, but they also contain the vitamins, trace elements, minerals and electrolytes such as sodium, potassium, magnesium, and phosphorus. You can have medical meal replacements and water and live on the moon with no other nutrition (until you get too thin). When patients in the hospital need to be fed through a tube, they are placed on medical meal replacement formulas. The ones used for weight loss are similar but taste better.

Because of the low-calorie plans, complete medical meal replacements are administered by a physician or other health care provider to ensure close monitoring. Weight loss is quite rapid and has a higher potential for side effects. These are very safe under the care of a medical provider but are very unsafe when used on your own.

Medical meal replacements can only be purchased from and need to be closely monitored by a healthcare provider. They provide all essential nutrients. Weight loss is fast.

If not monitored, you may develop electrolyte depletion and not know it. Under the care of a physician, this can be easily corrected with salt or potassium. Suffice it to say, if you see a soup, shake, or bar that you can purchase over-the-counter, it will be a non-medical grade meal replacement. In our experience, medical meal replacements are the fastest way to lose weight, with the exception of bariatric surgery. The reason is that by providing all the nutrients that you need on fewer calories and low carbohydrates, you feel less hunger.

Do I have to measure or weigh my food?

Whether or not you need to measure or weigh your food depends upon how well this procedure has worked for you in the past. Keeping a food journal improves mindfulness, making you more aware of what you eat. It is a means of controlling and tracking calorie intake, and can be an effective way to reduce calorie intake. Those who keep food journals while eating "regular" food are more successful at losing more weight than those who do not.

For those who are highly analytic, tracking calories may work well. If measuring food and tracking calories has not worked for you in the past, we do not recommend you measure your food. Many of our patients have been on diets that required weighing and logging their food intake but found this strategy ineffective in losing or maintaining weight. Measuring and logging was hard for them, and most discontinued the practice within a few days.

If you prefer to measure or weigh your food, two of the applications to consider are MyFitnessPal® and LoseIt®. Some patients also use a notebook. When using apps, some may scan barcodes from food labels or save your most common meal choices so that you can easily and repeatedly enter the data.

Why can't I eat regular food?

The better question is: what does "regular" food mean? One-third of Americans have obesity, and one-third of Americans are in the overweight range eating regular food. Therefore, eating "regularly" like everybody else will likely lead to either being overweight or having obesity.

Each person's plan needs to be individualized. If eating whole food works for you, then eat whole foods. Most likely, if eating whole food works for you, you will not be reading this book.

Can you control food intake while eating whole food? Can you reduce your calories, get all the nutrition you need, still be satisfied, lose weight, and also keep it off? The answer depends upon what regular food means to you. If you are eating "regular food," and you come into a weight loss center, it means that the "regular" food you have eaten and the way you have been eating is not working for you. Regular food in the past several years is more often processed and more often comes in a box. Usually that means it is refined with less nutrients and higher carbohydrates. In essence, regular food has contributed to an exploding obesity crisis.

In a perfect world, we would all eat three to four meals per day which we cook on the stove from scratch. That will take 30 minutes to cook per meal. In the 1950s, families spent over two hours a day cooking their meals. Currently, total food preparation and total cooking time averages 30 minutes per day. Some experts suggest we only eat foods that our grandparents would recognize. Oatmeal used to contain raw oats and required a 30-minute cooking process on the stove. That is not the 2.5 minutes or less that we currently spend when microwaving it. To make oatmeal that cooks in 2.5 minutes, the manufacturers precook it. This allows it to cook faster, but unfortunately, also modifies the oatmeal to release sugar faster as you digest it.

Do microwave ovens cause obesity?

As far as we know, microwaves themselves do not adversely affect your food, but they may be contributing indirectly to the obesity epidemic. When microwaves ovens became mass-marketed in the 1970s, Americans learned to reduce food preparation and cook time. We have become conditioned to expect a meal in two and one-half minutes from start to finish. Hunger often passes if we allow it to.

However, if we satisfy our hunger immediately, we do not allow time for the hunger to pass. As a result, rapid food preparation can actually lead to increased food intake.

The role of meal replacements in food addiction.

If you have food addiction, consider using meal replacements. Food addiction is the compulsive use of food which activates the reward centers of the brain. For example, some people use food to self-medicate feelings of depression. The eating of high carb foods releases serotonin and dopamine in the brain. The result is a brief feeling of well-being and pleasure. This pleasant feeling quickly disappears, often leading to shame or guilt. If you use food as a drug, you will tend to keep using the same drug. That's like the alcoholic saying, "Why can't I just have one drink?" or an ex-smoker saying, "I want just one cigarette." Once an addict stops the addiction, total avoidance is the only option, since one small relapse can quickly spiral into renewed addiction. The brains of addicts are forever changed and the reward pathways are fixed. Cravings reduce over time as long as they are not reactivated by even a single relapse. While food addicts cannot avoid food entirely, they can control cravings by reducing addicting foods laden with sugar, salt and fat.

Meal replacements give people a break from having to make difficult choices while providing the fuel and nutrients they need. They provide a needed interruption until a person has done the emotional work that may be needed to successfully manage having more food choices. Meal replacements help food addicts break maladaptive eating habits, since these replacements reduce the tough decisions of having to say "no" to unhealthy and tempting foods.

In conclusion, making the right nutritional choices is difficult. With so many options, it can be difficult to choose the best path toward weight loss. However, when working together with your weight loss physician, you can find the option that fits with your life-style, budget, and weight loss goals.

Danny: "Now that I've been through the program, I can't even ingest ranch dressing! I'm so much more aware of not just the calories and the fat, but also the other chemicals. I'm much more in touch with what I'm consuming and what the ingredients are. And, now I'm able to have a splurge, like a cocktail or chips at the Mexican restaurant, but I balance that with other choices I make during the week. When we have big family gatherings, I know that after a meal with a cocktail and a dessert I'll need to include four or five meal replacements the following day to get back on track."

Chapter 5: The Third Leg: Activity

DANNY: "MY DAILY activity was extremely limited, and I generally avoided exercise or outdoor activities. At night I found myself dozing off on the coach while watching TV because of all the food and carbs settling in at the end of the day.

"I hadn't considered what an important part activity played in my weight loss and more importantly, in weight maintenance."

The third leg in our four-part comprehensive weight loss program is activity. Exercise has many benefits that contribute to overall health. For example, all movement has a beneficial effect on mood, and we will discuss why physical activity in its many forms is essential for a weight loss program. You may be surprised at what constitutes exercise, how even a small amount can make a significant difference, and how over-exercising can also be problematic.

Isn't the answer "exercise more"?

Surprisingly, exercise alone is rarely a large component of weight loss. Exercise is critical for weight maintenance but by itself is a small part of weight loss. The truth is patients can lose weight without exercising at all; but without exercise they are rarely able to keep that weight off. We estimate that 80 percent of weight loss is related to how much you eat, with 20% related to exercise, assuming adequate sleep.

How much exercise is enough?

"Do I need to exercise 30 or 60 minutes to gain benefit?" The good news is that even ten minutes of activity has benefit. One of the greatest obstacles to regular exercise is the belief that it must consume a large part of your day. We recommend starting small with exercise. Set a goal to be active for one or two minutes a day. Every one or two workouts, add a minute or two until you are at 30 continuous minutes of exercise. If you enjoy your exercise, you can increase the time from there. Once you get into the habit, you may find that you no longer despise movement. The point is, you do not have to love activity in the beginning, yet you must do it. If exercise has not been a big part of your life thus far, keep searching for the type of physical activity that you can live with, tolerate, and maybe even enjoy.

In our experience, once someone has been exercising regularly for 30 to 60 days, they often find that they appreciate how they feel and want to exercise more and more. If you have a hard time getting started, begin by setting small goals; go easy on yourself. Take a walk to the end of the street or to the end of the driveway. Stand on the treadmill, and get off. It's a start. Working on frequency of exercise is the most important key, followed by increasing the duration of exercise. Ultimately, you should work up to 20 to 60 minutes per day.

Once you have increased your duration, you can then increase the intensity of your exercise. But again, this component should be last. People who do too much high-intensity exercise too soon increase their risk of injury. Limit high-intensity exercise to 10 to 20 percent of your overall activity.

Many people are successful using walking as their sole activity. Almost everyone can walk, and studies of long-term weight managers show that most of them use walking as their only activity. They cover at least 10,000 steps daily, equivalent to 20–25 miles per week.

Is there such thing as too much exercise?

Exercising too much can be as much a problem for weight loss as not exercising. Over-exercising, either doing too much or at too high an intensity can drive appetite upward; it is very easy to eat more calories than are burned.

On an aggressive meal replacement plan, you can do roughly an hour of moderate exercise per day. If you decide to do more than that, your doctor will need to increase your caloric and protein intake.

Some people who run marathons cannot control their appetite. The exercise is just too much. If they are not concerned with weight loss, many runners in marathon training can eat nearly all they want. Unfortunately, when they reduce training, they continue to eat the same amount of food, leading to rapid weight gain. Karla gained six pounds in six weeks after stopping marathon training while still eating the same amount of food that she had eaten when running. Heavy exercisers get used to eating so much during the training season that they are unable to dial down the intake when the season is over. Former pro-athletes often suffer from this problem (Charles Barkley, Shaquille O'Neal, and Roger Clemens are notable mentions). Finding the right balance between exercise and diet is key to successful weight loss.

Activity for Weight Maintenance

The amount of exercise required to maintain weight loss averages around 2500 calories of exercise burned per week and includes any movement: both intentional and non-intentional exercise.

Intentional exercise is what we do at the gym. This may involve activities such as walking, jogging, biking, and weight training. It can also include activities away from the gym, such as dancing, yoga, roller-skating, hiking, and playing team sports such as basketball or soccer.

Other ways to burn calories are non-intentional activities, in which our primary purpose is not exercise per se. These activities are called Non-Exercise Activity Thermogenesis (NEAT). A few examples of NEAT are parking your car farther away from your destination, walking up a flight of stairs instead of taking the elevator or escalator, or standing at your desk throughout the day instead of sitting. As other examples, plumbers, gardeners, painters and other manual laborers get much non-intentional exercise as they spend generous time bending, lifting, and stooping.

Yolanda is a loving grandmother and housekeeper who sought our help to lose weight. She dreamed of being thinner but had never been successful. She thought she needed to go to the gym to lose weight. Her diet consisted of rice and tortillas, and was low in fruits, vegetables and lean meats. She often skipped eating during the day, and had a voracious appetite in the evening. We had her wear a pedometer, which revealed that she walked 15,000 to 30,000 steps daily—which is the equivalent of seven to 15 miles!

For Yolanda, exercise was not her problem. Her level of NEAT was more than enough, but the stress of long days and meal skipping caused her to overeat at night. We placed her on a structured meal plan, eating protein every 2 ½–3 ½ hours, and added the weight loss medication phentermine to help her manage portion sizes and cravings. She lost 45 pounds, and has kept it all off for 10 years through continued meal planning, eating throughout the day so she does not get so hungry at night, and long-term use of phentermine. She was relieved to find she could spend her precious time off with her family rather than going to the gym!

You may have barriers to becoming active, and it is your doctor's role to help you find an activity that works for you. Cynthia told us that she hated to exercise. When we inquired further, she advised us that every time she exercised, she hated the feeling of sweat against her skin since it resulted in skin abrasions and skin irritation. When we asked what sort of clothes she was wearing, she told us that she was wearing cotton clothing. Simply changing from cotton to athletic wicking polyester fabrics freed Cynthia from this feeling, and she was then able to exercise. She found exercise was no longer uncomfortable and actually began enjoying a regular workout routine. For each patient, there are many reasons why one may not want to exercise. With patience and persistence, anyone can discover the joy of being active.

Which exercise is best?

The best exercise is the exercise that you like. The more you like the exercise, the more likely you are to do it. And if you dislike the exercise, you will dislike the time that you spend doing it. Unfortunately, when you detest the exercise you may need to find other ways to reward yourself. For example, if you force yourself to walk on the treadmill for three miles, burning 300 calories, you might compensate (consciously or unconsciously) eating high-calorie foods that contain more than 300 calories. We tend to overestimate the amount of calories we burn exercising and underestimate the amount of calories we eat.

To define a bout of exercise, or at least cardiovascular exercise, you need at least ten minutes of continuous movement. Any movement will do. If you like exercise of all types, then choose exercise that includes both cardiovascular (cardio) and strength training. Cardio includes running, swimming, biking, dancing, and hiking. The second type of physical activity is strength training: weight lifting, exercise bands, Pilates, and resistance exercise machines. For most, strength training is recommended for at least two days a week, and cardio the balance of days.

There are some people who just do not like exercise. They tell themselves stories that justify their feelings. We have found some people who say during the work week, "I'm just too busy to exercise." So we respond, "Can you exercise on weekends?" When it's a weekend or other time off work, what do they say? "I'm just too busy to exercise." They only learn later that vacations and weekends are more enjoyable when they are active, and that exercise improves their ability to manage the stress of work or family life.

Fear or reluctance are natural responses when contemplating an activity program. Prior experiences with overly aggressive trainers, embarrassment from mandatory runs during high school physical education, fear of failure, fear of pain, and shame from lack of fitness can all be reasons that you may not want to get started. We know you *will* have the courage to overcome these obstacles, and with great support you can accomplish more than you believe possible.

Can't I just exercise and not diet?

Exercise is believed by some to be the absolute way to lose weight. They exercise at the gym for 30 minutes two to three days a week and expect miracles. For example, two small sandwich cookies contain 106 calories, and walking a mile also burns the same. Most of us can eat two cookies in 15 seconds and will walk a mile in 20 minutes. Therefore, if we eat six cookies, we have to walk for an hour. If we eat 12 cookies, we have to walk for two hours and so forth. There just isn't time to completely use exercise to lose weight.

> *The simple truth is you cannot outrun a bad diet.*

The reason for exercise during weight loss is not just for weight loss, but also for all the other benefits. Exercise helps us feel energetic, helps clear our head, helps improve symptoms of depression and anxiety, makes us feel happy and calm, helps us sleep better, and lowers our appetite, to just name a few. While diet is the greatest factor during weight loss, exercise and diet are equally important in maintenance. In other words, physical activity elevates in importance during weight maintenance. Keeping exercise as part of a lifelong habit is essential for overall health.

Does sleep—or inactivity—play a critical role in weight loss?

It seems counter-intuitive, but you lose weight during adequate restorative sleep and gain weight from sleep deprivation. You must experience sustained periods of sleep if you want to lose weight and keep it off. There are several reasons why sleep deprivation leads to weight gain.

- **First, sleep deprivation leads to lower levels of leptin, the hormone that increases metabolism and raises fullness.** Lower leptin levels lead to overeating and decreased metabolism.

- **Second, those who are sleep deprived (less than seven to nine hours per day) have higher levels of ghrelin and as a result, they become hungrier.** Again, your hormones will work against you if you aren't giving your body the sleep it needs.

- **Third, sleep deprivation leads to higher levels of cortisol.** Excess cortisol leads to elevated blood sugar. Elevated blood sugar leads to an excess of insulin, which results in fat storage. High levels of cortisol also lead to deposition of fat around the belly and reduced muscle mass in one's extremities.

> *Sleep 7-9 hours each night to ensure optimal fat burning.*

In summary, patients will not lose weight if they get inadequate sleep, even if they follow their diet and get adequate exercise.

Sleep is probably the most overlooked component of a weight loss plan. Dieters often blame the wrong kind of dietary change, a poor metabolism, or lack of exercise as a reason for not losing weight, yet they ignore the importance of sleep. Although diet and exercise obviously are key components, they are not the only keys and do not work on their own.

One study on sleep showed that people who sleep less than seven hours are more likely to have overweight than those who sleep more than seven hours. In another large study on women who slept only five hours, 80 percent of them were found to be overweight. In another study, individuals' calorie output was measured at varying amounts of sleep. When these individuals slept for 5.5 hours or less they burned 400 fewer calories per day compared to those same people sleeping 8.5 hours. Sleeping an extra three hours has the same effect as running four miles per day!

Optimal sleep duration also decreases the appetite so you can more easily adhere to a nutrition plan. When your diet is in control, you tend to have more energy and can exercise better. When you exercise better you tend to sleep better. The process is circular and reinforces itself.

Fred worked for a company based in Europe. When he balanced his diet, exercise, and sleep, he lost weight. At times, he had conference calls at odd hours of the night, sometimes 2:00 or 3:00 in the morning, disrupting his sleep. If he kept to his diet and exercise yet got less sleep, he at least maintained his weight. Other times he would get plenty of sleep and exercise, yet not cut calories as much, and he was still able to maintain his weight.

Over the years we have found that people must have nutrition, activity, and sleep—in balance. With only two of them, people tend to maintain weight; with only one of them, people tend to gain weight; and with none of the three, people unfortunately tend to gain weight quickly.

Danny: *"Now, I'm much more active than I ever have been. At work I try to walk around more—just being mindful of my activity during the day. I park so that I get some steps in and take the stairs instead of the elevator. When I get home, Margaret and I will get another walk in with the dog, or go for a hike, or even take a yoga class. We also walk on our treadmill. We're not exercise fanatics, but we do include more movement in our daily life.*

"And I'm sleeping better. No more snoring. I feel rested and ready-to-go when I get up in the morning."

Chapter 6: The Fourth Leg: Education

THE FINAL COMPONENT of a comprehensive weight loss program, in addition to nutrition, activity, and medical management, is education. Individuals who have been chasing diets for their entire lives will need to learn new habits and understand the basis for their challenges. Through classes and one-on-one coaching with a weight loss physician, individuals can learn how to overcome old habits and create new ways to address age-old obstacles.

Here is a list of some of classes that we have found to be essential for weight loss:

1. How to manage emotional eating and eating when stressed
2. How to live a happy life (and how healthy eating can be a part of that)
3. Managing low self-esteem and poor body image
4. Sparking your motivation
5. Defeating food addiction
6. Building the diet that works for you
7. Shopping for and preparing healthy meals
8. Planning for successful social and vacation meals
9. Becoming a mindful person
10. Designing an exercise program that works for you

In this chapter we'll cover some of the topics that we address with our patients' education around weight loss, including breaking bad habits, understanding emotional eating, and dealing with plateaus. We'll also discuss living life in the midst of weight loss and maintenance by addressing social situations and vacations.

What are the benefits of classes and who teaches them?

The benefits of classes are many: the most important being greater weight loss. Our patients who complete our class series lose 44 pounds on average at one year, which is twice as much weight as people who attend no classes. One way classes work is by helping patients identify their food triggers. Classes help patients be mindful of portions and of the stresses around them.

The qualifications of class instructors can dramatically impact patient experience. The most qualified instructors are Ph.D. trained psychologists (doctors of psychology) and registered dieticians (RDs) with additional training in weight management.

Classes teach how to manage emotional eating, an issue ignored by most people who attempt weight loss. Emotional eating is the use of food to make one feel better, rather than eating in response to the physical need for food. One type of emotional eating is stress eating. People will often experience some degree of stress, and people will always need food. The problem occurs when stress and eating mesh together and interfere with each other. Psychologists help people create boundaries between food and stress. The combination of expert psychologists and qualified dieticians is invaluable in giving patients the tools to permanently keep off the hard-earned weight they have lost.

How do you help your patients break poor eating habits?

Emotional eating is using food—especially high carbohydrate foods—to relieve feelings of anxiety, depression, anger, low mood or low self-esteem. Characteristically, stress is low in the morning hours and builds throughout the day. Eating simple carbohydrates causes a surge in serotonin and other hormones, relieving stress, albeit temporarily. Simple carbohydrates are digested in 20 to 30 minutes, after which the serotonin decreases. When stress returns, so does the desire to eat. Unfortunately, the benefits from stress eating are always temporary.

In this way food is used like a medication. But as with any medication, there are potential side effects, and the side-effect of emotional eating is weight gain.

There are several tools used to treat this. First, classes help patients to learn to identify stress as it is happening instead of attributing these feelings to hunger. By understanding the cause of stress, patients can find healthier ways of managing it. For example, journaling thoughts, taking a bath, calling a friend, engaging in a craft or hobby, and exercising are all helpful in managing stress. Waiting 15 minutes before eating unhealthy foods allows the cravings to pass, a technique called "urge surfing." Weight loss medications help to decrease hunger and cravings when those methods do not help. In some cases, individual counseling is needed. Patients should be sure their weight loss center has psychologists available when needed.

Stress, meal skipping, and weight gain

One of the most important components to weight loss is getting nutrition throughout the day. We recommend eating every two and a half to three hours, getting exactly what you need when you need it. We call this "just-in-time nutrition." What does that mean? It means eating the proteins, essential fatty acids, vitamins, minerals, electrolytes, trace elements and fluids that you need throughout the day and at regular intervals. Unfortunately, many of these nutritional components are not stored anywhere in the body and therefore cannot be used later. So, for example, if you only eat once per day, your body will take what it needs for its immediate needs and turn the rest into fat. Also, if you go hours without eating, you will cannibalize your muscle protein reserves to maintain normal body function and repair.

Meal skipping is, unfortunately, a common stress response. We often forget to eat or ignore early feelings of hunger when under duress. The adrenaline surge of a highly stressful situation temporarily decreases our appetite. When you eat every two and a half to three hours, you prevent extreme hunger levels. However, when you go many hours between eating, overall calorie consumption may markedly increase when you finally do eat. You may also eat faster and eat much more food than you would if you were eating every two and a half to three hours.

How do I understand hunger?

Fullness scales are an excellent way to help manage food intake. They teach the all-important skill of mindfulness. Judging fullness or hunger does not come naturally to most people. On a scale of one to ten, starving is a score of one—at which point a person would even eat foods normally considered distasteful. Five is neither full nor hungry: This is where most of us should spend our day. On the opposite end is ten, at which point a person would not even eat favorite foods if offered. We recommend you score your hunger throughout the day, and also at the beginning, middle, and end of a meal.

As a general rule, do not wait to start eating until you are overly hungry. For example, we recommend that people start to eat when they reach a four on the scale. Also, we do not recommend overeating to the degree that one is too full. Instead, we recommend finishing meals at a fullness level of six or seven. Using this scale, a person should be satiated or comfortably full for three hours but also unable to go significantly past three or four hours without eating.

People with obesity often spend much of their day at the extremes of the scale. When the average person is asked, "When do you stop eating?" the answer is typically, "When I am full." Usually, when we are full, we have overeaten. The signals that tell the brain to stop eating are delayed by 20 minutes. The best example of this is when you leave the parking lot of one of your favorite restaurants and you rub your belly, feeling you have eaten too much. That discomfort occurs 20 minutes after you stop eating when the hormonal signals have had a chance to reach your brain.

The Japanese, with much lower rates of obesity have a mantra to prevent overeating. While eating, they say to themselves "hara hachi bu," which means 80% full. This is probably one of the reasons Okinawa is one of the Blue Zones.

Additionally, skipping breakfast, a common time when some people are not hungry, often leads to greater intake later in the day. Numerous studies have shown that the consumption of breakfast reduces overall food intake for the day, reduces hunger, and prevents overeating at nighttime. In other words, the habit of eating once per day is a strong source of weight *gain*.

> *Eating protein at breakfast is important to reduce excess night-eating.*

What are other issues affecting weight gain?

New patients are typically laser-focused on what they eat. They know what they have for breakfast, lunch, dinner, and snacks. When we start to address diet with our patients, we like to change the focus. We focus on *why* someone is eating, not only *what* someone is eating. A successful weight loss program goes well beyond just completing a food journal.

Emotions play a very significant role in eating. Are you overeating because you are happy, sad, lonely, bored, tired, stressed, depressed, anxious, having a good day, a bad day, starting a new job, or possibly losing a job? These are all common reasons why a person might be making certain choices, and these choices may have nothing to do with physical hunger. When we start to focus on the "why," we can substitute other habits for food. If you are tired, take a nap; if you are bored, find a stimulating and creative hobby.

What happens when I hit a plateau?

When someone loses weight and then stops losing, we call this a plateau. Plateaus occur for several reasons: decreased adherence to a plan that had worked in the past, decreased sleep, or a decrease in metabolism that occurs during weight loss.

When you begin a diet, it is probably because you are so miserable that you would do anything to lose weight. You are at the peak of motivation. As you lose weight (even a small amount), you feel better. The "pain" that prompted you to lose weight decreases, so you start to cut corners. You start eating out, drinking more alcohol, and snacking at night—things you never would have done when you started. These all lead to a significant slowing or stopping of weight loss. Ghrelin surges ensure you are hungry, which makes following your diet even more difficult. See Chapter One for more information on hormonal changes with weight loss.

At times, patients start skipping meals, eating just two or three times per day (expecting that by eating less frequently they are improving their chances at weight loss), or eating more carbohydrates. This is a another common time to hit a plateau. We've learned that eating protein more often (not less often) is the key to weight loss when coupled with the right nutrition, especially fewer carbs. A calorie is not just a calorie.

A decrease in metabolism with weight loss is another reason for a plateau. As we lose weight, our leptin levels drop, causing decreased satiety and a drop in metabolism. This change, along with the increasing ghrelin, means that keeping off weight is difficult on your own.

At 49, Lucy successfully lost 25 pounds through the use of a meal replacement meal plan and phentermine, but after six months her weight loss stalled. She began to have trouble dieting, but no matter what she did, she did not see the scale move. Stress from running a family sometimes caused her to turn to cookies in the evening. She did her best to get eight hours of sleep, but found that also to be a challenge. Due to lack of time, she was not able to exercise. At that time, we added metformin, which immediately reduced her cravings for sweets. After several months of weight plateau. Her weight loss resumed, and she reached her goal weight. One year later, she remains at that weight. She remains on phentermine and metformin, and finds that stopping either medication triggers weight regain.

You can overcome plateaus. A plateau is a time to reevaluate goals. If you have already accomplished everything you wanted to when you started your plan, you might consider setting a new goal. In some cases, like Lucy's, the addition of a second weight loss drug controls gaps in appetite control.

Also, as discussed earlier, lack of sleep is another common reason for a weight plateau. Sleep is an underappreciated component of weight loss.

What is a weight block?

Some people tell us, "Every time I get to X weight, I just stop losing weight" Those people have a weight block.

A weight block happens for conscious and subconscious reasons. For example, Jim believed that when he got to 175 pounds, something magical would happen: finding the perfect girlfriend. Mike thought that he would surely have that new job when he reached his goal weight. Sue had planned to run a marathon when she was close to goal. When these individuals got close to their "weight block" number and realized that they had not found the perfect girlfriend, landed the new job, or run the mini-marathon, they sabotaged their weight loss.

To overcome this hurdle, we keep patients off the scale. Once they quit looking at the number, they resume weight loss. If the goal by weight loss is to have a new job or a new significant other, patients are hanging the wrong requirements on weight loss. Weight loss makes one healthier and leaner, but it may not get patients a new job, a significant other, or a marathon tee shirt. Weight loss may, however, give patients the confidence to try new activities and become more social.

Childhood trauma can be another reason for a weight block. In the Adverse Childhood Experiences (ACE) Study from the Kaiser Weight Loss Clinic in San Diego, a score was based on the number of stressful childhood experiences to which participants were exposed. The questionnaire examined emotional and physical neglect, the presence of domestic violence to a parent, substance abuse in the household, parental divorce, neglect, and sexual abuse. Higher scores were associated with poor physical health, depression, anxiety, and obesity. This study has many applications in weight loss.

Sexual abuse is not only a common cause of severe obesity, but it is also a cause of weight blocks or plateaus. Some individuals with prior history of sexual abuse associate a large body size with the ability to create a safe space so as not to attract sexual advances. They consciously or subconsciously use weight to avoid dating and become uncomfortable when weight loss causes others to be interested. As patients confront these issues, we advise maintaining (rather than continuing) their attempt to lose weight. This allows patients the opportunity to do the emotional work with a psychologist. When they are emotionally ready and feel they have established safe boundaries, weight loss can resume.

One of the reasons for adverse childhood experiences causing weight issues as an adult may be that long-term stress causes dysfunction in the appetite centers of the brain (hypothalamus and pituitary gland). Childhood emotional trauma may permanently damage the brain.

Ultimately, while patients may not receive a specific promise they will reach an immediate weight loss goal, the vast majority of people who receive treatment by a certified obesity medicine physician, attend classes, begin to exercise, take weight loss medications (if needed), follow their meal plan, and communicate challenges to their provider will see dramatic life and health-changing weight loss.

What happens when I go away on vacation or have social meals?

Individualizing a plan for you is one of the most important parts of success. This is what personalized medicine is all about.

Many people go on vacations, have special work-related events, or go on cruises in the middle of a weight loss plan. A solid plan will help patients navigate this process. For example, there are certain things patients can do in the planning process that will help to maintain weight, even on a cruise. For example, meal replacements can be a very useful tool for between-meal snacks to prevent people from overeating. In other words, continuing to eat every two and a half to three hours, even while away, will prevent the inevitable hunger that occurs from starving oneself and then overeating at that meal. A little bit of planning goes a long way.

We recommend special planning for social meals called "preloading." Preloading is the process of having a protein snack or a meal replacement 30 minutes to an hour before the meal. Your mom told you, "don't eat before your meal because it will spoil your appetite." We want you to spoil your appetite! We want you not starving when you begin a meal.

We recommend that you begin the meal with two glasses of water and a large salad and skip the bread (push it to the other side of the table, out of reach).

> *Preloading is premeal planning. 1. Eat protein one hour before a special meal. 2. Begin the meal with two glasses of water. 3. Eat a large salad with low-calorie dressing or vinegar.*

Following this, move onto the protein portion of your meal. By filling yourself up with healthy food, you will be less likely to overeat unhealthy food.

Next, decide what your expectations are regarding your weight while on a vacation or a cruise. Would it be your goal to limit your weight gain to two or three pounds? If that is your plan, then that's what you will accomplish. If your goal is to maintain your weight on such a trip, then you will most likely do that. We certainly do not encourage our patients to aim for weight loss during those times. This is a good opportunity to practice the use of long-term tools.

Are you an all-or-nothing thinker?

Try living in the gray zones rather than living in a black and white world. Gray zones mean that you adjust your expectations based upon your situation at the time. There are times when our patients lose 20 or 30 pounds and then times when other areas of their lives become a higher priority. When that happens, we aim for weight maintenance until patients can focus on weight loss and are ready to re-engage.

The all-or-none approach does not lead to success. Life is more like a dimmer than an on-off switch. When we follow a diet perfectly, we feel in control. Unfortunately, stress can cause us to eat foods we said we would never eat again. That often leads to guilt and shame, which kills willpower. With those feelings, we often abandon our diet and eat recklessly. Then on

Monday we recommit to dieting. That is an all-or-none philosophy, and it is defeating.

We suggest that you think more like a dimmer— which can be bright or dim but never off. When you start the day, your "light" is at 100 percent. If you do happen to eat a snack that is off your plan, it may only bring your light down to 92 percent. When you eat more of that food, your dimmer goes down to 85 percent, but then you go for a walk or run, and it goes back up to 90 percent. When you wake up the next morning you are back at 100 percent again. Put yesterday behind you; today is a new day and a fresh opportunity to learn, grow, and become a successful weight manager. The goal is to not be too strict on yourself. Be forgiving, and don't go completely off the diet. That is balance. Focus on today.

The point is to find a plan that is individualized to your life and is consistent with your long-term goals. When deciding what you will do on vacation or at a social meal, you have to sit down and decide for yourself what your goals are. Many people decide that weight loss so important, that they will remain on the same diet. A green salad with vinegar is always acceptable, as is drinking sparkling water with a lime instead of an alcoholic beverage.

Each person finds tricks that work for him or her. Rachel worked in sales, which required she entertain clients for dinners. In advance, she would tell the bartender, "Every time I order vodka on the rocks, I really want water and a lime." Everyone around thought she was drinking vodka. This gave her the control she wanted without making a scene, and allowed her to avoid peer pressure.

Sometimes you may choose to suspend your plan and accept possible gain weight. There is probably no food that we will tell you never to eat. No matter what the food is, it will have a recommended frequency and a quantity. You can either eat a small amount of it on a regular basis or a large amount of it on a rare basis. Eating pizza is an example: if you had one slice of pizza occasionally and did not lose control, that is great. We call that a "treat" rather than a "cheat." If you eat a square of dark chocolate but have it regularly, every day or every few days, it is much better than eating a whole bar.

> *Guilt and shame reduce willpower. Eating unhealthy foods can be called a "treat" rather*

There are some important things to do on vacation to ensure success. The first is to get adequate sleep. When sleeping in a different bed, in a different room, in a hotel, you may not sleep as well as you do in your own home. It may take longer to get to sleep, so you will need more time in bed to meet the seven-hour goal. The second issue relates to hydration. When you get dehydrated your appetite increases, so drink lots of water. A bit of planning goes a long way to ensuring success on vacation.

Paul, an engineer, benefited from a structured approach. Shortly after starting his program, he began frequent work travel. He often ate dinner alone in a restaurant. In the past, he would either eat all of his large-portioned meal or take leftovers back to his hotel. Later he would eat the leftovers. Early in his treatment he learned to reduce the effect of travel on his diet. When eating out, he would ask for an additional plate. He would take all of his food, cut it exactly in half (the engineer in him) and put the other half on the second plate as soon as his meal came. He would then ruin it in one of two ways. The first was to pour water on it. The second was to pour an obscene amount of salt or pepper on it. This made it impossible to eat the rest of the meal. This continued for six months. After building the habit of eating smaller meals, he was then able to ask for a bag at the beginning of the meal, wrap up half, take it to his room, put it in the fridge, and successfully eat it the following day for lunch.

What emotional support should I expect?

Emotional support is critical during your weight loss journey. Sometimes we get asked if starting the program with a spouse, significant other, or family member is good idea, and the answer is a resounding "yes." Weight loss is contagious! Roger and Jackie had a practice that worked for them. They said, "We never both have a bad day at the same time." They had an agreement: if one was having a bad day and wanted to eat something off the diet, then they would talk to the other, who often was not having a bad day. They found that by encouraging each other they were able to achieve their goals together.

There are many ways to gain emotional and psychological support. The more sense of support and connection to community that you have, the better you will do in weight loss. In our clinic, for example, group-led classes can be a great source of support because they give you the tools to become a lifelong weight manager and create community while working toward shared goals. Our psychologists give one-on-one support when needed.

Also, support groups work by surrounding you with other like-minded individuals who are on the same journey. Online support groups add additional support and can be accessed through social media. We use a private group on Facebook, which has created a buddy system of nearly 300 patients who are available 24 hours per day. We have found this online support group to be invaluable in helping our patients achieve long-term goals by sharing successes and challenges.

Emotional support should be multifaceted. It should come from your physician and office staff, making your visits to the clinic comfortable. Even the furniture can create a positive and encouraging environment. Firm chairs of appropriate size, large blood pressure cuffs, and large gowns communicate to patients that the entire staff is sensitive to your needs.

Finally, emotional support should come from the people in your life. Your physician can help you find the right words to talk to loved ones and friends about how they should act when food is available, or when you are losing weight.

Chapter 7: Your Weight Loss Journey with Weight Loss Centers

WE BELIEVE ALL who suffer from obesity should be treated with compassion and respect, and that those who seek treatment are heroes.

Now that you understand the four critical elements of a comprehensive weight loss program, let's talk about what you can expect as you work with an obesity medicine physician in a weight loss center.

What should I expect at a weight loss center?

When you call the office of a weight loss physician, you should expect understanding and empathy for your disease. We treat obesity as seriously as we treat any other serious condition, including cancer.

The most difficult part of this journey is making the call. We know that in the past, many patients have been chastised by their physicians, family, friends, and loved ones and are left to feel guilt and shame because they have not been successful in losing weight. Lack of success is often taken as a personality flaw.

Many patients initially feel intimidated by the process before they make the call for an appointment. After that call, patients feel a sense of relief, and more importantly, they finally feel understood and that there is hope for a plan that will work for them. Some of our most successful patients were also the most skeptical when they initially called us. They expected their experience to be just like every other: eat less, move more, and deal with the hunger. Fortunately, those who call will quickly understand that we have a different approach.

Through the right program patients not only feel great during their weight loss, but they also feel more successful than they ever have in the past. We are inspired by that glimmer of hope we see after our patients achieve initial weight loss and continue on their journey to success.

What should I expect from my first visit to a weight loss center?

When you call the office, you may be offered an appointment to see the provider at the onset, or you may be offered an orientation, or informational consultation. The latter is an overview of that particular center's approach. We favor the latter. At this session, you will have an opportunity to tour the office and meet with staff to learn their approach. These services can be offered in a group or on an individual basis. Most importantly, you will have an opportunity to ask questions.

Questions you should ask:

- How often will I see the physician?
- Do you use vitamin injections or HCG (Note: we advise against HCG as we've discussed, and "fat-burning" shots are ineffective)?
- Do you prescribe weight loss medications?
- What are my meal plan options?
- Do you offer classes? Who teaches them? What are the teachers' qualifications?
- What are all the costs involved?
- What costs are nonrefundable, if any? Are there long-term contracts or commitments?
- Do you use meal replacements and may I taste them?
- What is your maintenance plan?
- Do you track patient results?

- What results can I expect?

> *It helps to write down your questions so you do not forget all of your concerns.*

Next, your weight-loss journey will begin. The staff, often medical assistants, are trained in taking blood pressure and pulse, drawing blood, and doing EKGs, and doing blood work to get you started. Labs are important to evaluate for medical conditions that may impact your care.

At Scottsdale Weight Loss Center, for example, we perform the following tests:

- **Electrocardiogram (EKG):** looks for damage to the heart or changes in heart rhythm. This is especially important, since some of the medications used for weight loss can increase metabolism, thus increase the heart's need for oxygen. Some EKG changes will alert the physician that a patient should undergo stress testing or be referred to a cardiologist prior to starting those medications or high-intensity exercise.

- **Comprehensive metabolic panel**: preferably fasting (nothing to eat after midnight before the test) is used to evaluate blood sugar for diabetes, kidney function, liver function, and electrolytes. With testing we can diagnose conditions like prediabetes and fatty liver disease.

- **Thyroid function testing**: indicates whether thyroid is under or over-active. A low thyroid will decrease metabolism and contribute to obesity.

- **Cholesterol testing (LDL, HDL, and triglycerides)**: helps us determine risk of heart attack and stroke. Many patients with obesity have elevated cholesterol. Weight loss often improves these risks dramatically.

- **Complete blood count**: evaluates for anemia; general signs of poor health; and deficiency in iron, B12 or folic acid.

- **Uric acid**: helps determine if a patient is at risk for gout, which can flare during weight loss. Very high levels of uric acid will lead to painful crystals forming in the joints of the feet. If the level is elevated, medication can reduce that risk.

- **Hemoglobin A1C** (Hga1c): a test for diabetes and prediabetes.

In addition to testing, you will fill out a medical history form and diet and emotional trigger questionnaires to help your provider fully understand you. The physician will then tailor a plan that is safe and most effective for you.

In a medical program, the next visit will be with your physician. That visit will last 40-60 minutes, one-on-one, with a goal to discern the best plan for you. The first question typically is, "Why do you want to lose weight now?" Common triggers include special future events, high school reunions, or possibly a past experience that led to embarrassment regarding weight. After meeting with the physician, we take a thorough diet history. We ask about previous dieting attempts, what has worked in the past, and also, obviously, what has not worked.

The physician will review your medical history, medications, and surgeries and will then do a physical exam to assess for other medical complications. After this, the doctor will review and interpret your lab tests, and finally, your physician will design your personalized diet plan that you can start immediately. He or she will also discuss how often you will follow up—the critical feature of any successful program.

How often do I weigh in?

If you are on a doctor-prescribed plan that gives you everything your body needs, yet on fewer calories, trust the plan, and you will see results. Do not weigh yourself at home. While your weight will drop, weighing yourself too often may lead to frustration. One reason for this is that your body water fluctuates dramatically day-to-day, based upon factors such as salt and carbohydrate intake, urine, and time of day.

We find that weighing-in weekly is just about right and provides needed accountability.

There is no one-size-fits-all weight loss plan. With very rapid weight loss we may need to adjust or stop certain medications, so you may need to be seen more often. Later, you may visit less often. In our clinic we see patients weekly for the first 20 weeks of their program; then usually every other week after that.

How often do I consult with my physician?

Paul, a 62-year-old IT worker and semi-professional poker player has had weight gain since his 30s, and at one point, reached 205 pounds. He has high blood pressure and high cholesterol.

Nighttime cravings caused him to eat popcorn, nuts, or ice cream each night. Sometimes, he would get the motivation to diet, but each time he lost weight, he regained all the weight he lost. He has tried numerous diets, including Weight Watchers®, Nutrisystem®, and Jenny Craig®. What he learned is that each approach lacked the guidance and accountability he needed to be successful long-term.

When Paul came to our center, he felt embarrassed about the state of his health. His weight caused him to lose the ability to do normal daily activities that gave him joy, like walking. He chose a full meal replacement program, because "I can't trust myself to make healthy choices right now." Over the next four months, Paul dropped 48 pounds, normalizing his blood pressure so that he could discontinue his antihypertension medications. He came in for a weigh-in each week, and met with his physician every two weeks. After four months, he started to visit his physician twice per month.

After a year of maintenance, Paul now comes in every month. He chooses to do this because he knows he needs that level of accountability. Prior experience has shown him that he regains weight when left on his own. He feels if he were to stop frequent visits, he would make poor food choices and stop walking, both important for weight maintenance.

When you go to an obesity medicine specialist, the frequency of visits will be determined by many factors.

For example, if you want to lose weight more quickly or have many medical problems, you will need to meet with your physician more often. In general, a visit each week leads to the most success. The longer patients go between visits, the less accountability they have. Patients tend to follow their plan because they know that they have to get on the scale at their next visit.

There is a difference between weighing yourself at home and weighing yourself at your doctor's office. When you get on the scale at home, your doctor will not be there to see your weight. It helps to think of your doctor as your secretary of health and human services, but you are still the boss. That is gentle accountability: you are in control and there is no guilt.

When weighing at the office, the physician will be there to encourage and to guide you back to achieve the results that you want to achieve. Ultimately, you are the driver of your treatment plan, and your goals are most important. These goals are not your doctor's goals. Your weight loss center and your weight loss physician are your tour guides. The two are always there to help you achieve the results that you want to achieve.

Once you have reached your weight loss goal, patients do best when they are seen once to twice a month.

This should continue for a minimum of 12 to 18 months.

What results should I expect?

Of course, as physicians, we want you to become healthier. When you lose five percent or more weight, it is considered medically significant. At five percent, blood pressure starts to drop and blood sugar will also begin to begin to decrease. As you hit 10% weight loss, blood sugar will likely normalize, blood pressure (if still elevated) will further drop, and if you were on blood pressure medicines, you probably will be able decrease some or all of them. If you have a strong family history of hypertension you might still need medications despite attaining a normal weight since genetic hypertension does not respond to weight loss. At 10% weight loss, sleep apnea improves and LDL cholesterol starts to improve. By the time you lose 15%, you will experience even further cholesterol and metabolic benefits.

Patients feel better within a couple of weeks on the right plan. Feeling better is a sign of a successful plan. The whole goal of a weight loss plan is to burn fat, which should start by day three. One of the fastest areas to improve is knee pain. Each step at your initial weight puts great strain on your knees. Just losing 10 pounds takes approximately 25 pounds off your knees with each step (2.5x your weight), and 20 pounds of weight loss takes about 50 pounds of weight pressure off your knees with each step.

Each person's weight and overall health goals are personal to them. Your goal may be to lose a certain number of pounds or to obtain a certain clothing size. If your goal is strictly to attain a weight number, you should discuss whether your expectations are realistic or not. An effective weight loss plan should lead to safe and effective weight loss. We know that losing as little as five percent reduces your risk of diabetes and high blood pressure by 50%. Most medical programs lead to weight loss of between 10 and 15% of total body weight, which is 30 pounds in a patient who weighs 200 pounds. Highly motivated patients can achieve weight loss of 20-30%. Some of our patients have reduced their weight by half!

Some people have a goal to reduce medications. This goal is certainly achievable with weight loss. Reducing medications is actually one of the reasons we changed from primary care in which we spent much of our time putting people on drugs for ailments linked mainly to obesity. We know that if patients can overcome obesity, we can happily take them off many drugs. For example, many patients on insulin are able to discontinue injections within one to two months of beginning weight management treatment.

Another result that you may hope to achieve is to be able to complete a bucket list goal. For example, do you want to run a 5K or a marathon? Do you want to hike the Grand Canyon? Do you want to complete a cancer walk, or do you want to hike Machu Picchu? If those are your hopes, they certainly may be achievable. An excellent weight loss physician will help design a plan to help you achieve those dreams.

Is faster better?

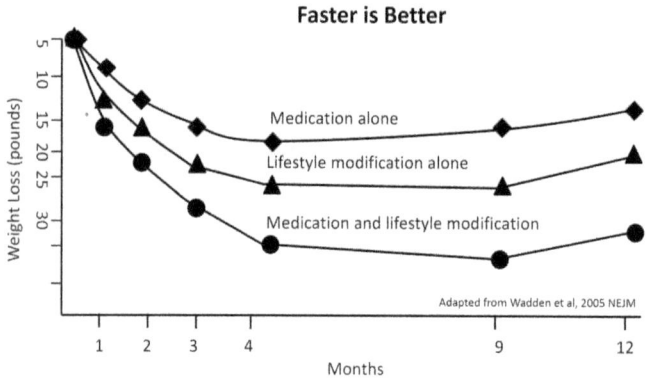

Weight loss interventions of varying intensity are shown. In the top line (diamonds), weight loss medication is used alone. In the middle line (triangles), lifestyle modification is used alone. In the third line (circles), medication is combined with lifestyle modification. This shows that the group that lost the most weight in the first 1, 2 and 3 months of treatment also weighed the least at 12 months. Early fast weight loss results in the most weight loss at one year.

The truth is, as long as you receive complete nutrition, the best way to lose weight is to lose it quickly. Weight loss studies that show more rapid weight loss in the first several months leads to greater weight loss at one year, and in several studies the weight lost at one and two months predicts the amount of weight loss at one year, four years, and eight years. Why is this? Those who lose weight more quickly will likely stay more motivated. They feel better more quickly, and they get off their medications more quickly. In addition, faster weight loss reduces hunger the most. The most aggressive diets contain lower calories and lower carbohydrates. Reduced carbohydrate diets lead to a release of ketones, which suppress the hunger hormone, ghrelin. The faster you lose weight, the more your body releases breakdown products of fat that suppress appetite.

In studies of weight loss, six months is a common time to plateau. So, the more you lose by six months, the greater weight loss you will have overall. Truly, early success in losing weight predicts further success.

We are just starting to decipher the genetics of obesity and how people's genes affect weight loss. We know there are some people with obesity who, no matter what diet plan, medication, or exercise, will lose quickly while others on the same plans lose more slowly. We believe this is the definition, not of obesity, but of obesities. Obesities are different genetic diseases that manifest with the phenotype (appearance) of obesity or overweight. Just as there are many types of cancer, there are many types of obesity.

Do you offer any types of guarantee of weight loss success?

Beth, a 42-year-old computer sales account rep stated at her first visit to our center, "I cannot lose weight." Most of her meals were eaten with clients or on the go. She rarely ate at home. She had tried "every diet," and none of them had produced any weight loss. She advised us that losing weight would be a "miracle." We told her we could certainly help her lose weight and were so certain she could lose that we placed a five-dollar bill on the counter that she could keep if she failed to lose weight. She passed this symbolic guarantee at each visit. After losing her first 20 pounds, she said, "OK, you win. You get to keep your five dollars!"

The simple answer is yes to a guarantee in nearly all cases. A good physician will guarantee to take all of his or her knowledge and experience to help a patient lose weight to the best of the physician's ability. In our experience, 90% of patients lose weight quite quickly, and 10% percent lose weight more slowly than expected. These are the patients who most need a comprehensive program, including close accountability, support, classes, and weight loss medications. Patients can reach weight-loss goals, but the journey will be slower.

Reasons for slow loss can include:

1. **Slow metabolism**: This can be caused by advanced age, menopause, small body frame and sarcopenia (low lean body mass). Weight training and stimulant-based weight loss medications can help.

2. **Unfortunate genetics**: Some people whose bodies are exceedingly good at storing fat, have "thrifty genes." This may have served their ancestors well in times of famine.

3. **Sleep deprivation**: Discussed in Chapter 5 on activity, even the best weight loss plan can be sabotaged by lack of sleep.

4. **Medications such as insulin, beta blockers, blood pressure medications and prednisone**: Talk to your physician about alternatives when available.

At Scottsdale Weight Loss we do something different. We take the focus off the scale, at least initially. We ask how your clothes are fitting (looser), if you are hungry (no), and if you have increased energy (yes). These are all early indicators the program is working. Many people have been weighing themselves every day for years, and it obviously has not helped them.

What should I look for in the qualifications of a medical support staff?

Critical to your success is surrounding yourself with people who help you achieve your long-term goals. Not only will you be working with a medical provider, but the staff at the office are also an important part of your support group. Those trained in medicine such as medical assistants and nurses will be a significant part of your journey. They not only measure your vital signs, but also are individuals with whom you can develop a trusting relationship throughout your journey. They bridge the gap between you and your physician.

It takes a long time for staff to attain excellence in weight loss support and empathetic understanding of patients' feelings and needs. Medical assistants in our practice take six months to be very good at what they do and a year to be able to function independently. A great office will invest abundant time developing staff that supports and empathizes with you. During your program, you will get to know the office staff quite well, so it is important that they are professional, friendly and accommodating.

What happens if I do everything I'm asked to do, and I'm not successful?

We find it rare that a patient doesn't lose weight. This usually happens when patients underestimate how much they are eating and overestimate the amount of calories they burn through exercise. Additionally, the consumption of hidden calories ("sneaky calories") may inhibit weight loss. For example, alcohol, nuts, and coffee creamers are common sources of calorie intake that people do not properly measure.

Some patients eat large amounts of food and aren't even aware of it. This is called mindless eating. An important component of successful weight loss is to become more mindful. Another reason patients may not lose weight is that they self-sabotage. If patients are overly harsh with themselves, they may rebel and overeat.

An additional reason for lack of weight loss is overestimating the amount of calories that one's body requires. If a woman is in her 50s and is five feet tall she may only have a calorie budget of 1100 calories per day. That is the amount of calories she needs to eat each day to maintain her weight. What does this mean? She has very little leeway for calorie intake, and for her to lose weight, she must reduce her calories markedly. She may be surprised that she has not lost weight in the past despite diligently following a diet. In truth, she has been following her diet; she has just been giving her body more fuel than it actually burns each day.

What is the cost of the program?

The first question you need to answer is not the "cost" but what is the "value" of the program. A comprehensive program has many components. If your plan involves physician care, it will be costlier, but you will also lose weight more quickly, safely, with less hunger, and with fewer complications. With physicians, you will have access to medications and a more aggressive diet which should be easier to follow. A physician will guide you, reduce blood pressure and diabetes medications at the correct times, and will give proper counsel on diet and exercise.

High-quality behavior-based classes add to the cost of the program but will also double the weight loss. In our practice, we offer special classes and support groups. All of these together create a comprehensive program on which it is difficult to attach a set value.

Another way to answer the cost question is to ask how much you have actually spent on other programs so far that have not worked for you. Some programs may have been cheaper, but failure is even more costly. Lower cost=lower value.

You have to also look at how much you are spending on the food that you currently eat. How much are you spending at Starbucks® each day? A blended drink could cost six dollars and have 600 or more calories. Do you eat out for lunch (costing 10 to 20 dollars per day)? Dinners out are even more expensive. Are you having alcoholic drinks? Meal replacement plans actually save significant money versus the cost of eating whole food and eating out.

The least expensive diet plans are those that you do completely on your own. Next are those run by peers. A costlier approach is through a medical practitioner. Finally, surgical obesity treatment is the most expensive. Finding the one that best fits your needs is very personal.

Is the program covered by insurance?

In many states obesity treatment is specifically excluded. Insurance companies often have "*carve-outs.*" Carve-outs are specific medical conditions that are not covered by your plan. This is determined by your health insurance or employer. One can attempt to seek reimbursement from the insurance company; unfortunately, as of the writing of this book, most insurances do not cover weight-loss services. In Arizona, for example, few insurance programs cover weight-loss services. In a few states, such as California, insurance is more likely to cover treatment.

An excellent option is to receive reimbursement from a *medical savings account (MSA)*. These are plans in which you set aside pretax money by your employer allowing you to pay for health care expenses. Medical weight loss services, labs, and classes are all generally covered by MSA accounts. You can ask your employer if such a program is available on your plan.

A bill in Congress, *The Treat and Reduce Obesity Act*, does offer hope for obesity treatment coverage. This act, if and when approved, will require insurances pay for weight loss treatment including medications. Unfortunately, despite being introduced in three sessions of Congress and with over 100 sponsors, the bill is yet to be voted upon. Be sure to watch current legislation on weight loss issues to find out about positive changes as society comes to see obesity differently.

Do I have to sign a contract?

Understanding the financial agreement early in the process is an important part of your research. We suggest you avoid "golden handcuffs": paying for services up front without the ability to stop if the program is not working for you. We believe that your program has to be right for you; if not, you should be able to cancel at any time.

Danny: *"It's funny. While I've struggled with my weight my entire life, coming to the weight loss program and working with the physicians and team has been one of the easiest things I've ever done. I wish I had made that decision a long time ago. I know it helped that Margaret and I did the program together, too.*

"In the first week I lost seven pounds. And I recall thinking, 'This is going to work!' While I was skeptical for the first few weeks, my steady weight loss helped me feel motivated and optimistic."

Chapter 8: Maintenance and Beyond: How to Keep it Off!

What is the best maintenance plan?

JOANIE HAS BEEN able to lose 20 to 30 pounds, but each time she lost in the past, she would quickly regain. She found it easy to stick to diets for two to three months, but found she tired of them. She tried Atkins®, Medifast®, and Weight Watchers®, but the more she lost, the more her hunger increased. During a previous attempt, her primary care doctor placed her on phentermine, which controlled her appetite and made adhering to her diet much easier. After losing the weight suggested by her doctor, he told her she needed to stop the medicine because it "wasn't safe" to continue. As soon as she stopped phentermine, her appetite increased, and she rapidly regained.

For many, stopping an effective medication is not the answer. Joanie was relieved to hear that while the FDA only approved phentermine for use up to 12 weeks, best practices supports ongoing use if the benefits outweigh the risks. If monitored carefully, Joanie may stay on phentermine forever, just as many do for treatment of other chronic diseases. Most of our patients check in every one to two months while on medications for weight loss. Joanie has not experienced any side effects on phentermine, and the risks of obesity far outweigh any potential risk of medicines.

The best maintenance plan is one that keeps the weight off, helps people live a happy lifestyle, results in better health, and frees patients from the hunger that often occurs after weight is lost. We use the term "**active maintenance**" to refer to a long-term treatment plan. Weight loss requires an active plan, a very specific plan for patients to lose weight. Active maintenance is a plan to keep the weight off, specific but less restrictive than the weight loss plan. In active maintenance, we recommend that patients weigh frequently, at least once a week. Many maintenance patients still choose to weigh-in daily. Patients arrive at a weight they want to maintain for the rest of their lives. We tell patients to "**never buy bigger pants**." If they don't fit, it's time to change what you are doing to fit into the old pants.

We use green, yellow and red zones to help you to determine where you are in your active maintenance journey and any changes you need to make to stay within your green (healthy weight) zone. If your goal weight is 150 pounds, your green zone should be within two pounds of that number. For example, you should maintain weight between 148 and 152 pounds. If your weight ever hits 153-154 pounds, you are now in the yellow zone, and should proceed with caution. The first step is to resume the meal plan you used to lose the weight, reduce eating out, eliminate alcohol, ensure at least seven hours of sleep nightly, and increase physical activity. **If you gain five pounds above your goal weight, you are now in the red zone.** We recommend a **visit with your doctor as soon as possible** to help you get back on track.

Active Maintenance: Keeping It Off

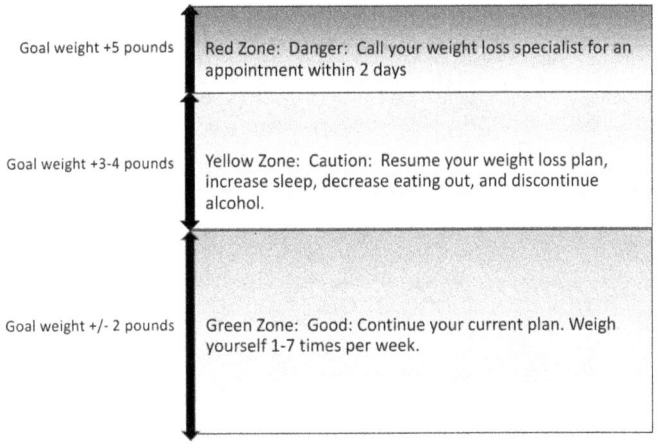

When regaining weight, many people experience guilt and shame because they feel like failures. They tell themselves they should be able to keep the weight off by themselves. These feelings, while common and understandable, are not productive. Patients tell us the more they try to lose weight on their own, the more they feel like failures. This leads to further feelings of guilt and shame and the cycle continues. Our advice is to get in to see your doctor as soon as possible, because you didn't lose weight on your own and you are not expected to keep it off on your own. In other words, try to overcome any internalized feelings of guilt and shame and put them behind you so that you can get back on track as quickly as possible.

We find when patients gain five or more pounds, they tell themselves, "I do not want to come back into the office until I have gotten down to just the five pounds above my goal." More often than not, this approach backfires. When patients finally do come in, sometimes it is after gaining ten or more pounds, a larger gain to overcome.

During maintenance, weigh yourself at least once per week. Have a plan if you gain three pounds or more.

The best maintenance plan is a comprehensive approach, along with a physician who helps to find the ultimate plan that you can stick with for the rest of your life. Instead of serial dieting, aim to become a lifelong weight manager. In maintenance, weight may fluctuate. You may deviate from your target weight goal a bit. It may go up a couple pounds; it may go down a couple pounds, but the goal of a lifelong weight manager is control. If your weight increases, you will learn to analyze the factors in your life that led to your weight increase. Whether a stressful situation, family vacation, lost job, or some other stressor, you can learn how to regain control over your weight.

Other components of a maintenance plan include ongoing emotional support to help you navigate through the many stresses of life. You must learn to identify your food triggers in order to successfully handle vacations, boredom, and stress. Many people use food as a drug, eating high carb, high-fat foods to temporarily quell feelings of anxiety, depression, or loneliness. It takes much learning and practice to understand how to deal with these feelings in a healthier way.

The National Weight Control Registry is the largest database of successful weight managers. (http://www.nwcr.ws/) To be included in this registry, you have to lose at least 30 pounds and keep it off for at least one year. The registry began in 1994 and now has over 10,000 members. This registry shows that there are certain consistent factors that occur before people regain weight. In particular, the most common trigger for weight gain is a sudden drop in exercise. Paradoxically, when people exercise less, they tend to eat more, further accelerating the weight gain and producing feelings of guilt and shame. However, our job is to quickly help you get back on your weight loss journey as a lifelong weight manager.

One of the areas of controversy in weight loss and weight maintenance is the long-term use of weight loss medications. Approximately 50% of our patients use these medications long term. What does that mean? It means that to keep weight off, a patient might need to take these medications for life because any time patients stop these medications, they may see weight gain. There is no one best choice. It is the job of your physician to help you decide which medication is best and safest for you.

How long does maintenance last?

Keeping weight off requires an individualized plan that works, along with personalized guidance from a weight loss practitioner. Maintenance includes many components. The first component is regular monitoring, both on your own and with your doctor. We recommend monthly follow up for a minimum of 18 months following weight loss.

Danny: *"This is the first time that I've lost weight and maintained it, and it has changed my life. Buying clothes that fit was always a tough thing for me, and I was always self-conscious about how I looked. Looking at old pictures is painful; I can see that I was always trying to find clothes that camouflaged my weight. Now, I don't have these issues!"*

Chapter 9: Success!

"BUT I KNOW what to do." This is what patients tell us every day. They know what to do; they just can't get themselves to do it. This can be for many reasons. It may be a plan that has not worked for them, and in many cases, it may be due to a lack of motivation. Everybody seems to know what to do: eat less and exercise more. However, this approach almost never works. Our job is to help turn you from a chronic dieter into a "weight manager." The truth is that you may know what to do, but you may not know *how* to do it.

Many of our patients are "professional dieters." They are experts at counting calories, carbohydrates, and fat—even better than many dietitians—but the simple answer is that if this plan was working for them (counting calories, carbs, etc.), we wouldn't be having this conversation. They repeatedly, yet unsuccessfully, try to lose weight. Support and education are crucial to figuring out what is best for each person and how to troubleshoot special situations. You can learn from others via sharing and learning how to plan: the most important tool.

People will make mistakes when dieting. Mistakes are part of the education process- the goal is to learn from them. There is much self-discovery on the road to becoming a weight manager. Dr. Primack's favorite food in the world used to be cake. Now, when he is at a birthday party and someone hands him a piece of cake, he has learned that the simple answer is "no thank you." It took abundant practice to get to this point. He has learned not to say, "I'm on a diet," or "I keep low carbohydrate," because then there's always a comeback. The cake pusher says, "Just have a little one" or "Just this time will be OK." *What is OK* is for each person to decide for themselves.

What are your other triggers? Is ice cream, cookies, or cheese and crackers in your home? When you are unstressed, you may be able to avoid eating those foods. In times of stress or lack of sleep, these foods function as drugs. There is a reason people use the term "sugar rush."

When looking at a weight loss program, you should make sure you are not just being provided a diet without any additional support. If you enroll in such a program, you may lose some weight but probably not more than 10 pounds. Even more important, you may have a great deal of difficulty keeping off the weight.

How successful is your weight loss program?

When selecting a weight loss program, results are what matter most. An experienced weight loss center collects data on weight loss. It will measure your weight loss throughout the journey. One-year weight loss statistics are one of the most important early measures of success. It is great to see lots of weight loss in the first one or two months because that says the program that you are on can help you lose weight, but what matters most is the ability to maintain that weight loss.

For example, at Scottsdale Weight Loss Center, our patients with a BMI of between 35 and 40, lose on average 36.2 pounds at one year. Those who have a BMI of 40-45 lose an average 47.4 pounds at one year. We are hard-pressed to find results that rival these figures, other than bariatric surgery. In a 2005 JAMA study, several do-it-yourself diets and one-year weight loss figures were compared. The best of those diets, Weight Watchers, and Zone, showed a loss of 6.6 and 7 pounds, respectively. The fact is that on these diets, you can lose a few pounds on your own, but we don't think seven pounds (nor should you) is significant enough to warrant the effort.

Success may also be defined in other ways. Should you expect to feel better during your weight loss program? Patients in a medical weight loss program see rapid improvements in overall well-being and mood. The reason is that while patients are losing weight, they are also getting complete nutrition, as well as emotional support to help them achieve this meaningful change. Most of those people dieting on their own will not see the improvement in health that a comprehensive medically supervised weight loss program can deliver.

Patient satisfaction is another important measure of success. There is no point in losing weight if you are miserable in the process. In our clinic, we closely monitor our patients' feelings of well-being, as well as hunger throughout the process. For example, after the first week of the program, we ask our patients if they felt the program was harder, easier, or as expected.

Around 90% of patients tell us it is easier, 5% say as expected, while 5% state the plan is harder than expected. In these patients, stress is a common reason for difficulty. Sometimes because of stress, they stop the program for a period of time, and sadly, some will turn to more trendy diet plans. Often patients come back because they learn through the process that our program does work for them, and they are ultimately more successful. Also, if you fall off our weight loss plan, or stop coming in for a while, we make it very, very easy to return. It is a rule that we do not chide our patients for the very simple reason that they've already been too hard on themselves. There is no benefit to making anyone feel even worse. No one plans to have obesity.

More Success Stories

We want to leave you with hope—hope that you can stop chasing diets forever and find a solution like so many of our patients.

In these final pages, we want to leave you with hope and inspiration by sharing some of their stories.

Tom's Story

I'm pleased to share my story about how I lost 53 pounds in 20 weeks with the help of the staff at Scottsdale Weight Loss Center. My dentist lost about the same amount of weight, and he inspired me to go check out the program. I have spent most of my life struggling with my weight. I, like most people with weight issues, had tried many do-it-yourself or over the counter weight loss options. Every year, year after year, I would be up a few pounds, hating myself and feeling hopeless. If you are reading this review, then I would assume you have concerns about your weight, health, and quality of life. If you are like me, you just want some information to make an informed choice as to whether this program will work for you or not. It's OK to have a healthy skepticism about these types of programs ... I sure did. It took me a full year after I went to hear about the program to join up. In my opinion, you are doing the right thing by reading about other people's experiences before making a final decision.

Here are some of my personal experiences and observations:

1. I found the facility to be professional, comfortable, and nicely decorated. There is a nice reception counter, offices, exam rooms, and seminar rooms, all conveniently located in the same building.

2. My initial meeting was with the patient coordinator. I think you will like her right away; I did. The thing I liked about her was her pleasant personality, knowledge about the program, and her professionalism. Later, I found the whole staff to be friendly, professional, and highly supportive.

I always feel very comfortable, calm, and welcomed when I go to the center.

3. The doctors are REAL MD's with REAL credentials. Dr. Primack was my doctor, and I found him to be soft-spoken, kindhearted, highly educated, understanding, a great listener, excellent advisor, and always available for me when I had questions or concerns. I have heard that Dr. Ziltzer is the same.

4. I received all the information about the program without being pressured in any way. You will be given all the information to make an informed decision as to whether the program is right for you or not. I felt that they truly wanted me to make the choice, based on my desire and reasons, and to commit to the program and be successful. Ultimately, weight loss is a personal choice and not something that can be imposed.

5. The patient coordinator explained the costs involved, which I found to be accurate and reasonable. She explained how the program works and what I could expect; there were no hidden costs. Most importantly I learned about the maintenance program, which is what finally sold me on joining. Just a note about cost: I know this can be a sticking point for

many people. I personally came to realize that if losing weight was only about money, I was not ready to seriously lose the weight and keep it off. I had to get to the point that I had to do something about my weight, no matter what it cost. Just remember, when calculating the cost, to take into account the cost of not losing the weight, the cost of medications, doctor visits and co-pays, the cost of food it takes to maintain your weight (eating out more, higher grocery bills, for example), the cost of low self-esteem, and feeling lousy every day. Now that I'm through the program and realize where I was and where I am now, I can honestly say it was the best money I ever spent and I totally got my money's worth and more.

6. My initial medical evaluation with Dr. Primack was excellent and thorough. My program was personalized to my lifestyle and needs. My health was closely monitored throughout the four-month program.

7. One critical part of the program was the educational component. The seminars with the dietitians and clinical psychologists was invaluable and provided the support and long-term tools needed to maintain my weight loss success.

Finally, I learned to stop rewarding myself with food, punishing myself with food, avoiding things like boredom, work stress, past life experiences by medicating myself with food. I now eat for my health and understand exactly what I'm putting in my mouth and how it affects my weight, health, and quality of life.

Don't be afraid of the OPTIFAST® products. They really work to lose weight fast, plus you will receive a lot of valuable information from OPTIFAST® on losing and maintaining a healthy weight. I think the products taste good, and they really worked for me. One of the hardest things I had to deal with was looking at myself in the mirror and seeing a different person. It took a while to get my head around it. By the way, plan on buying a new wardrobe! Also plan on getting a lot of questions and attention about your new image. I encourage you to check out the program.

Chris' Story

After spending the last 13 years yo-yo dieting and never being able to keep the weight off, I was finally ready for a lasting change. I started the Scottsdale Weight Loss Center program and lost a total of 36 pounds in nine weeks! I did a full meal replacement plan and an appetite suppressant. This was the easiest plan I've ever done! I've been able to keep the weight off for the longest amount of time due to the awesome maintenance plan, which has been really easy to follow. Thank you!

Keri's Story

My weight loss adventure started over a year ago. I had just turned 42 years old and my weight had gotten out of control. Even when I was pregnant with three kids I weighed less. I worked out three to five times a week, but my eating habits were horrible. I had a very good friend who had lost over 70 pounds at Scottsdale Weight Loss Center, and she had kept it off for over three years. I finally got the courage to make my first appointment and mentally made a decision to change the way I felt and looked. I have lost over 50 pounds, and I am enjoying life to the fullest. My children have noticed a huge difference in me, not only in my weight, but also my higher activity level. The program was perfect for me. It taught me how to eat the correct portions and got me back on track to eating healthier.

Carl's Story

Before I started with the Scottsdale Weight Loss Center's program, I had prediabetes, and my blood pressure fluctuated from 140/92 to 136/92. I slept a lot and was tired most of the time. I didn't exercise regularly. I was frustrated and wore 2XL shirts, and my waist was a size 44. My cardiologist, during a routine exam, suggested the Scottsdale program for my wife and me, and I do believe that suggestion saved our lives. Now I'm 55 pounds lighter, wear size-large shirts, and my waist size is 36. I walk three to four miles daily with my wife, and I'm so much healthier and happier. Even more important is the fact that now I know how to manage a healthy weight and have the tools to cope with emotional eating.

Michael's Story

I found the plan to be very easy to follow, and I lost weight quickly and consistently. The classes have been extremely helpful in educating me about the choices I make and how to be successful at maintaining my weight. I have a new nickname: Skinny! I have always hiked, and I haven't been able to hike like I did when I was young until I lost the 50 pounds. After not reaching the top of Squaw Peak for almost 20 years, I now regularly make the summit. Dr. Primack and the staff have been fabulous. Thank you!

Mary's Story

I have been dieting most of my life. I was a fat kid who grew up to be a fat teenager who at the age of 15 decided she needed a diet to make her life better. Since then I have been on and off diets for years. In the last few years, I had just given up, thinking that I was just unable to keep the weight off. I figured that I just had to face it that I would live the rest of my life in the half of the world who were overweight. I had failed at that part of life. I was resigned to living that way until my doctor sat me down and told me I had borderline diabetes and I would have to go on blood pressure medicine for the rest of my life. I was not about to let that happen. I did my research and it led me to the Scottsdale Weight Loss Center.

In the past 20 weeks I have lost 52 pounds, an amazing number to me and my family. I did the work but I had lots of help. I mean lots and lots of help from all the staff at the clinic. The support team were there for me all the way, answering my questions, cajoling me along, and helping me be successful with this program. I can never thank them enough for their help; this was a completely transformative experience for me! I no longer have to worry about medical problems. I no longer have to avoid stairs, or make up excuses for not being able to tag along with my kids on long bike rides. I even went down a whole shoe size! This has changed my life in every way possible.

Having finished the [first five months of the] program, I was uncertain about what would come next—more of the program or transitioning to a full meal life. I was elated to find that whichever way I wanted to proceed

I still had all the resources of the Center. No just dumping me out to work this out on my own. The people that had come these 20 weeks with me would still be there to help meet my goals. That support will be vital with ongoing weight loss and transitioning. The fears I had about the future have evaporated. It is a wonderful feeling that they will still be there for me, whatever my future holds.

Again, there are so many ways this has changed my life—the list grows as I live a healthier lifestyle. And I will always be thankful that I took the chance and had the immensely talented, supportive, and caring team with me.

Rhonda's Story

I have tried many diets before, but when I got to the point of buying larger and larger clothes and looking at pictures of myself, I made the decision: It was time! I was now convinced by that little voice in my head and the constant lectures from my daughter—herself a personal trainer and nutrition specialist—that it was time to get healthy. As I got larger, I found I was having a difficult time breathing; walking any distance. I was drowning my misery in fattening foods.

I started to look online for a program and found another program that required an up-front fee and also required shots, and I decided to pass on that. When I learned about Scottsdale and made a visit, I was hooked and called to say, "Get me started!"

I began my journey in 2015 when I met Dr. Ziltzer and bought my food. I thought it was going to be difficult, but I realized it wasn't.

I hadn't seen my family or friends for several months, and when I did I was a little over halfway to my goal. My friends and family were so excited to see me. My sister, my niece, and friends all started crying and told me over and over how proud they were of me and how great I looked. No one had told me that for a very long time. When I visited my daughter in Dallas, she pulled up to the curb at the airport with her mouth wide open and started crying! She was so happy and made me feel so very good!

I am almost to my goal with about two pounds to go. I am eating regular food, but being very careful and mindful of what I put into my mouth. I still attend classes, which is very important. I'm also working out. I've had to take all of my clothes to either resale shops or donate them, and I am loving buying new clothes in smaller sizes. My daughter and sister are getting me new clothes and I'm loving every minute of it!

I can breathe! I haven't used my CPAP machine for four months now. I can go to the gym, walk for long periods of time without being winded and am feeling better than I ever have!

The staff at the Center is amazing! When I walk to the door, I feel welcome. Everyone is friendly and sincere.

I am convinced that this is not a "diet"—it's most certainly a lifestyle change that is comfortable. I feel I am reaching success! I recommend this program to everyone I talk with and who asks, "How did you do it?"

Cindy's Story

In the summer of 2017, I'd had enough: enough sleepless nights, enough heart issues, and enough inflammation and pain in my legs and joints that kept me from enjoying fun outdoor hikes with my family. I felt lost, discouraged, and overwhelmed. Was this all I had to look forward to after turning 60?

A friend suggested to me that she'd achieved success [at Scottsdale Weight Loss Center], and I was ready. A year later my life has changed in ways I never thought possible! I've shed the unhealthy 61 extra pounds I'd carried for years while regaining my good health and long-lost energy. I love the new clothing fashions, and this transformation has provided the perfect opportunity to swap out my now unneeded extra-large clothes for an all new extra-small sized wardrobe.

Those hiking trails that a year ago scared me now make me smile as I keep up with my family on adventurous hikes.

The physicians and the medical team at the Scottsdale Weight Loss Center were with me all the way. Make that decision to shed those unwanted extra pounds for YOU, not for your husband, job, doctor, or significant other … just for YOU … I promise you will be glad you did!

Kirk's Story

My weight loss journey started about a year before I came to the Scottsdale Weight Loss Center. I was tired of feeling and looking the way I did, and I did not like what I was seeing in the mirror every day. I started swimming for my exercise since high-impact exercises were not realistic for me. I joined the LA Fitness in South Gilbert and had to relearn how to swim in a more efficient way to aid in my weight loss. I was eating healthy, reading food labels and exercising, but I was still gaining weight. I couldn't figure it out so I made an appointment with my primary care doctor. I found that I had high blood pressure and high cholesterol and was given medications to treat the symptoms. I didn't just want to treat these conditions; I wanted to fix them!

I started investigating different weight loss centers, and a friend at work knew someone who had gone to Scottsdale Weight Loss Center. After I called and met with the patient coordinator, I realized that I could not do this on my own. The simple fact was that I needed medical help in a structured weight loss program.

I started using OPTIFAST® as well as Metformin in 2016. I have experienced other diets, but eating the four OPTIFAST meals a day with a whole food meal combined with metformin—my magic pill—allowed me to see immediate results. When I began, I was 275 pounds with 40% body fat, and by the end of my 22 weeks I lost 50 pounds. Every week I was losing weight. Seeing that continual weight-loss was a key for me to stick with the program.

At 225 pounds I was ready to expand my fitness plan. I was already swimming and added spin cycle to my cardio routine at LA Fitness®. I then added weight training to build muscle and increase my core strength by joining a gym called TI Fitness in Gilbert.

I read in MyFitnessPal about a man who lost weight and entered the world of male physique competitions. Now I'm the type of guy that if I don't have a goal, I will lose motivation. From his story, I found inspiration to enter men's physique competitions.

In 2017, I started an 11-month fitness plan to reduce my body fat and increase my muscularity. I tracked my frustrations and successes every day in an electronic journal called Day One, which I've published as an eBook. During this time my testosterone naturally increased from 627 to 713, a change of 13%, and my waist when from size 36 to a size 32.

I entered two men's competitions in 2018 weighing 186 pounds with 15% body fat and won third and fourth place trophies. At 55 years old I am in the best shape of my life.

I have grown a lot the last two-plus years, including finding a passion to inspire others. I have directly affected several individuals to start their own fitness journey with my Instagram postings. I am working toward becoming a certified personal trainer, and I'm creating a website to reach a wider audience to empower them to make healthy life decisions.

My advice to anyone looking to lose weight and get fit is to trust the process. It will be slow going and yes, I wanted to quit at times. But I didn't quit because I want to live a long, happy life and I knew if I followed the plan, I would attain my goals. It is okay to be selfish about yourself, to make life decisions that are best for you that may not be best for others in your life. You have to make the decision that the most important person is you and seek out a team of experts, from physicians to counselors to trainers, who will support you in the process. You cannot make a better you by yourself.

And don't think you cannot still enjoy food and beverage while losing weight. I am a foodie and enjoy craft beer to this day. You just have to learn the rules of moderation and balance, having fun with your quest to make you a better you.

Danny's Story

While you've heard Danny's story throughout the book, this is one of our favorite parts—his role as the "skinny" guy.

Air travel wasn't much fun when I was heavy. I always had trouble squeezing into the seat and buckling my seat belt, and it was embarrassing when the people sitting next to me readjusted themselves in their seats to give me the room I needed. Now when I travel, I don't even hesitate to take a middle seat (especially when I want to sit near the front of the airplane) because now I'm just as comfortable in the middle as I am in an aisle seat. It's funny, now I'm the skinny guy! I'm the guy that may need to scoot over to accommodate that heavier person sitting next to me. It's great being that new guy.

Your Story

Are you ready to stop chasing diets? Are you equipped to begin your final weight loss journey? Are you eager for more health and more happiness?

You can do it, but you should not do it alone. You need medical help and the proper plan to get you there.

We are ready to partner with you on this journey. Are you ready?

Suggested Reading

Our expertise comes from the research and training we have received from some highly dedicated scientists and clinicians. Without their hard work, we would never have been able to achieve such patient success. Our knowledge rests on their shoulders. There are a number of books we feel to be especially helpful to understand the disease of obesity.

Bray, George. *Contemporary Diagnosis and Management of Obesity and The Metabolic Syndrome*

Breus, Michael. *The Sleep Doctor's Diet Plan: Lose Weight Through Better Sleep*

Buettner, Dan. *The Blue Zones: Lessons for Living Longer From the People Who've Lived the Longest*

Kessler, David. *The End of Overeating: Taking Control of the Insatiable American Appetite*

Reynolds, Gretchen. *The First 20 Minutes: Surprising Science Reveals How We Can Exercise Better, Train Smarter, Live Longer*

Steelman, Michael. *Obesity: Evaluation and Treatment Essentials*

Taubes, Gary. *Why We Get Fat: And What to Do About It*

Westman, Eric. *The New Atkins For a New You*

Whitsett, David. *The Non-Runner's Marathon Trainer* (which guided both Drs. Primack and Ziltzer across the finish line the first time)

Reference Notes

"Adult Obesity Facts." *Centers for Disease Control and Prevention*. CDC, 2018. Web. 28 September 2018.

"The Adverse Childhood Experiences (ACE) Study." cdc.gov. Atlanta, Georgia: Centers for Disease Control and Prevention, National Center for Injury Prevention and Control, December 2015.

Beccuti, Guglielmo, and Silvana Pannain. "Sleep and Obesity." *Current Opinion in Clinical Nutrition and Metabolic Care*. 14.4 (2011): Web. 19 Sept. 2018.

Bischoff, S.C. et al. "Multicenter evaluation of an interdisciplinary 52-week weight loss program for obesity with regard to body weight, comorbidities and quality of life—a prospective study." *International Journal of Obesity*. 36 (2012): 614–624. Print.

Burfoot, Amby. "Biggest Weight Loss Myth Revealed." 2015. *Runner's World*.

"Cardiovascular Effects of Intensive Lifestyle Intervention in Type 2 Diabetes." The Look AHEAD Study Group. *N Engl J Med*. 369 (2013): 145-154. Print.

Casazza, Krista, et al. "Myths, Presumptions, and Facts about Obesity," *N Engl. J Med.* 368 (2013): 446-454. Print.

Clark, Cari Jo, ScD, Rachael A. Spencer, MPA, Susan A. Everson-Rose, PhD, Sonya S. Brady, PhD, Susan M. Mason, PhD, MPH, John E. Connett, PhD, Kimberly M. Henderson, BA, Michelle To, and Shakira F. Suglia, ScDf. "Dating Violence, Childhood Maltreatment, and BMI from Adolescence to Young Adulthood." *Pediatrics.* 134.4 (2014): 678-685.

Dansinger ML, Gleason JA, Griffith JL, Selker HP, Schaefer EJ. "Comparison of the Atkins, Ornish, Weight Watchers, and Zone diets for weight loss and heart disease risk reduction: a randomized trial." *JAMA* Jan 5 (2005): 293(1): 43-53.

"Diabetes Prevention Program." *National Institute of Diabetes and Digestive and Kidney Diseases.* NIDDK, US Department of Health and Human Services. Web. 20 September 2018.

Gangwisch,I. JE, Malaspina D, Boden-Albala B, Heymsfield SB. "Inadequate Sleep as a Risk Factor for Obesity: Analyses of the NHANES." *Sleep* Oct. 2005: 1289-96. Print.

Hendricks, Ed, et. al. "Addiction Potential of Phentermine Prescribed During Long-term Treatment of Obesity." *International Journal of Obesity* 38 (2014): 292-298.

Nedeltcheva, Arlet V. et al. "Insufficient Sleep Undermines Dietary Efforts to Reduce Adiposity." *Annals of Internal Medicine* 153.7 (2010): 435–441. PMC. Web. 19 Sept. 2018.

Noll, Jennie G., Meg H. Zeller, Penelope K. Trickett, Frank W. Putnam. "Obesity Risk for Female Victims of Childhood Sexual Abuse: A Prospective Study." *Pediatrics* July 2007: 61–7. Print.

Patel, Sanjay R. et al. "Association between Reduced Sleep and Weight Gain in Women." *American Journal of Epidemiology* 164.10 (2006): 947–954. PMC. Web. 19 Sept. 2018.

Shai, Iris, et al. "Weight Loss with a Low-Carbohydrate, Mediterranean, or Low-Fat Diet." *N Engl J Med.* 359 (2008): 229–241. Print.

Zilberstein, Bruno, et al. "Topiramate after Adjustable Gastric Banding in Patients with Binge Eating and Difficulty Losing Weight." *Obesity Surgery* 14.6 (2004): 802–805. Print.

About the Authors

Robert Ziltzer, MD, FACP, FAAP

"As long as I can remember, I wanted to be a physician. I was, and still am, always driven by the opportunity to make a difference in peoples' lives. I care for my patients as I would my family." Dr. Ziltzer attended Albany Medical College and residency in Phoenix, Arizona where he became board certified in both internal medicine and pediatrics. He began his medical practice in 1991 as an internal medicine and pediatric physician.

As a primary care physician, Dr. Ziltzer valued the long-term relationships he developed with his patients, but sensed a frustration that there had to be a more productive and transformative way to treat many of the chronic health issues his patients were facing.

"In med school they didn't teach us how to help patients lose weight, they didn't teach us how to treat obesity." To help these patients, he wanted something more than a prescription pad and a referral to Weight Watchers.

This lack of a more defined medical approach to weight loss and weight-related illness was something he related to professionally and experienced personally. His father, who was moderately overweight, suffered his first heart attack at age 52 and died from his second heart attack at 57.

In 2006, Dr. Ziltzer, along with Dr. Craig Primack pursued specialty training and became certified in obesity medicine, and introduced a comprehensive medical weight loss program in their primary care practice. The results were so dramatic, and the response by patients was so overwhelming that by the end of the year they transitioned out of primary care practice and founded Scottsdale Weight Loss Center.

"It is incredibly gratifying when I hear people tell me about the huge changes in their lives as a result of losing weight."

Dr. Ziltzer personally believes in healthy lifestyles, and became a marathon runner at the age of 41. He has completed 10 marathons, several half-ironman triathlons and one Ironman Triathlon. He has been voted one of *PHOENIX Magazine*'s Top Docs 12 times. He is a national speaker on obesity-related topics, and has a special interest in treating professional athletes.

Dr. Ziltzer is married, lives in Scottsdale and has two children.

Craig Primack, MD, FACP, FAAP, FOMA

When Dr. Craig Primack was home for winter break following his first semester of college, his father suffered a heart attack at the age of 52. He spent the winter break by his father's side, and by the time he returned to school he decided to change majors and started on the path to becoming a physician.

He went to medical school at Loyola University in Chicago, and moved from Chicago to Phoenix for his medical residency program in both internal medicine and pediatrics. He joined Dr. Ziltzer in private practice in Scottsdale in 2001, and they began focusing on weight loss programs. He became certified in obesity medicine, and realized he'd have the opportunity to change patients' lives through weight loss.

"When I realized that people were having real success and improving their health and lives through weight loss, I knew this was for me. Weight loss is a real way to make a difference in patients' lives."

In 2006 Dr. Primack and Dr. Ziltzer shifted their practice, focusing solely on weight loss by establishing Scottsdale Weight Loss Center.

Dr. Primack is now a nationally recognized expert in obesity medicine, serving for several years on the board of the Obesity Medicine Association (obesitymedicine.org), a clinical society of over 2200 physicians and other medical professionals. He will serve as the president of the Obesity Medicine Association from 2019-2021. He has appeared on the Dr. Oz Show several times to discuss weight loss topics. On one program in 2012, he introduced the first new weight loss medication released in 12 years, described as a "silver bullet" for weight loss. He regularly enjoys speaking to various medical groups around the US about obesity and weight treatment.

Dr. Primack has been voted one of *PHOENIX Magazine*'s Top Docs ten times.

Dr. Primack is a supportive physician and compassionate coach with invaluable expertise in helping patients improve their lives through proven, personalized and comprehensive medical weight loss.

When he's not helping transform lives in the office, he's helping shape them at home as a devoted dad to his three children. Dr. Primack is an avid road cyclist and runner having completed around 30 half-marathons.

To reach Drs. Robert Ziltzer, MD and Craig Primack, MD or for more information, visit: scottsdaleweightloss.com or email info@scottsdaleweightloss.com.

To schedule a patient consultation in Arizona, call 480-366-4400.